RELIGION IN JUDAH UNDER
THE ASSYRIANS

STUDIES IN BIBLICAL THEOLOGY

A series of monographs designed to provide clergy and laymen with the best work in biblical scholarship both in this country and abroad

Advisory Editors:

PETER R. ACKROYD, *Samuel Davidson Professor of Old Testament Studies, University of London*

JAMES BARR, *Professor of Semitic Languages and Literatures, University of Manchester*

C. F. EVANS, *Professor of New Testament Studies, King's College, London*

FLOYD V. FILSON, *Formerly Professer of New Testament Literature and History, McCormick Theological Seminary, Chicago*

C. F. D. MOULE, *Lady Margaret's Professor of Divinity in the University of Cambridge*

STUDIES IN BIBLICAL THEOLOGY

Second Series · 26

RELIGION IN JUDAH UNDER THE ASSYRIANS 732-609 BC

J. W. McKAY

ALEC R. ALLENSON INC.
635 EAST OGDEN AVENUE
NAPERVILLE, ILL.

© *SCM Press Ltd 1973*
ISBN 0-8401-3076-7
Library of Congress Catalog Card No. 72-97460

Published by Alec R. Allenson Inc.
Naperville, Ill.
Printed in Great Britain

CONTENTS

TO MARGUERITE

PREFACE

This book is based on one of the chapters in my dissertation, *Josiah's Reformation, its antecedents, nature and significance*, which was submitted to the University of Cambridge for the degree of Ph.D. in 1969. While examining the causes of the reformation, I became convinced that motivation for the Josianic purges was more religious than political and that religion in Judah under the Assyrians was not dominated, as has so often been assumed, by an obligation to venerate Assyrian gods in Jerusalem. Further research since the completion of my thesis has only strengthened this conviction.

I wish to acknowledge my deep debt of gratitude to Dr E. W. Nicholson for the encouragement and guidance which he has so generously given me, not only when he was supervising my research in Cambridge, but also in the years since. I should also like to thank the members of the Old Testament Seminar in Cambridge (1967-9) and Mr A. E. Goodman of the same University for their various criticisms and suggestions. I am greatly indebted to Professor P. R. Ackroyd of King's College, London, and to my colleague in Hull, Dr R. N. Whybray, for their comments on both thesis and manuscript and for offering so freely of their assistance in many ways. In particular my thanks are due to Professor W. G. Lambert of the University of Birmingham who with infinite patience and kindness has criticized my use of Assyrian and Babylonian materials, has drawn my attention to several important publications, and has offered many suggestions which have greatly improved this work. To these and to the many other scholars with whom I have discussed the subject-matter of this book I am much indebted.

I should like to thank Mr Jonathan Barry for checking the many references in the manuscript, and the staff of the SCM Press for their careful work in preparing it for publication.

I dedicate this book to my wife in gratitude, not only for specific tasks she has undertaken in connection with it, but for the patient encouragement and support which she has given me throughout all stages of its growth and without which the work might never have been completed.

University of Hull   JOHN W. MCKAY
January 1973

SOURCES OF ILLUSTRATIONS

The author wishes to express his indebtedness to the following scholars, institutions and publishers for permission to reproduce drawings and to make drawings from photographs:

The University of Chicago Press for figs. 4 and 7 from H. G. May and R. M. Engberg, *Material Remains of the Megiddo Cult,* The University of Chicago Oriental Institute Publications 26, Pl. xxi and p. 7, fig. 1, copyright 1935 by the University of Chicago, all rights reserved; Dr K. M. Kenyon and the Jerusalem Excavation Fund for fig. 5 from *PEQ* 1968, Pl. xxxvi. A; The Magnes Press for figs. 12b, 1b, 6, and 13c–e from Y. Yadin, Y. Aharoni, R. Amiram, T. Dothan, M. Dothan (not vol. II), I. Dunayevsky, J. Perrot, *Hazor II. An account of the second season of excavations, 1956,* The James A. de Rothschild Expedition at Hazor, 1960, Pl. clxiii.2, and *Hazor III–IV. An account of the third and fourth seasons of excavations, 1957–1958,* 1961, Pl. cccxv.1, cccLvi.1 and cccxLiii.29, 31, 35; The Palestine Exploration Fund for figs. 8, 13 and 20b from F. J. Bliss and R. A. S. Macalister, *Excavations in Palestine during the years 1898–1900,* 1902, Pl. 67.15s, 56.7, 14 and 56.44z, and for figs. 1a, 9, 16, 20d, 12a, 14f, 20a, c from R. A. S. Macalister, *The Excavation of Gezer, 1902–1905, and 1907–1909,* 1912, vol. II, p. 454 fig. 535, p. 442 fig. 524, p. 349 fig. 466, p. 296 fig. 438, vol. III, Pl. ccxxi.2, ccxxi.25, cc.36, cxc.59; Dr J. B. Pritchard for fig. 18 from *ANEP,* Pl. 792; L'Administration de la *Revue Biblique* for fig. 15 from *RB* 44, 1935, Pl. iv.2; Dr C. F. A. Schaeffer and the British Academy for figs. 2, 10, 11, and 14a, b, 17g, h from C. F. A. Schaeffer, *The Cuneiform Texts of Ras Shamra – Ugarit,* Schweich Lectures 1936, 1939, Pl. xv.2, p. 22 fig. 6, p. 49 fig. 10, and Pl. xxxii.1; The Wellcome Trust for fig. 17a–f from O. Tufnell, C. H. Inge and L. Harding, *Lachish II (Tell ed-Duweir): The Fosse Temple,* The Wellcome-Marston Archaeological Research Expedition to the Near East Publications 2, 1940, Pl. xxvi.9–11, 13–15.

Fig. 3 after W. M. F. Petrie, *Gerar,* Publications of the Egyptian Research Account and the British School of Archaeology in Egypt 43, 1928, Pl. xxxix.14; fig. 19 after Petrie, *Ancient Gaza, Tell el Ajjūl* I, Publications of the Egyptian Research Account . . . 53, 1931, Pl. xxviii.4.

ABBREVIATIONS

AB	The Anchor Bible, New York
AfO	*Archiv für Orientforschung*, Berlin
AHw	W. von Soden, *Akkadisches Handwörterbuch, unter Benutzung des lexikalischen Nachlasses von Bruno Meissner* (1868–1947), Wiesbaden, 1965ff.
AnBib	Analecta Biblica, Rome
ANEP	J. B. Pritchard (ed.), *The Ancient Near East in Pictures relating to the Old Testament*², Princeton, 1969
ANET	J. B. Pritchard (ed.), *Ancient Near Eastern Texts relating to the Old Testament*³, Princeton, 1969
AnOr	Analecta Orientalia, Rome
AO	*Archiv Orientální*, Prague
ASTI	*Annual of the Swedish Theological Institute in Jerusalem*, Leiden
ATD	Das Alte Testament Deutsch, Göttingen
BA	*The Biblical Archaeologist*, New Haven
BASOR	*Bulletin of the American Schools of Oriental Research*, New Haven
BDB	F. Brown, S. R. Driver and C. A. Briggs, *A Hebrew and English Lexicon of the Old Testament*, Oxford (1907), 1959
BH³	R. Kittel (ed.), *Biblia Hebraica*, Stuttgart, 1929–37
BHS	K. Elliger and W. Rudolph (eds.), *Biblia Hebraica Stuttgartensia*, Stuttgart, 1968ff.
BJRL	*Bulletin of the John Rylands Library*, Manchester

BKAT   Biblischer Kommentar – Altes Testament, Neu-
                  kirchen
BWA(N)T   Beiträge zur Wissenschaft vom Alten (und
                  Neuen) Testament, (Leipzig), Stuttgart
BZAW   Beihefte zur *Zeitschrift für die Alttestamentliche
                  Wissenschaft*, Giessen, Berlin

CAD   I. J. Gelb and others (eds.), *The Assyrian Diction-
                  ary of the Oriental Institute of the University of
                  Chicago*, Chicago, 1956ff.
CB   The Century Bible, Edinburgh
CBSC   The Cambridge Bible for Schools and Colleges,
                  Cambridge
CBQ   *The Catholic Biblical Quarterly*, Washington
CIS   *Corpus Inscriptionum Semiticarum*, Paris, 1881ff.
CML   G. R. Driver, *Canaanite Myths and Legends*, Old
                  Testament Studies 3, Edinburgh, 1956
CRAI   *Comptes Rendus de l'Académie des Inscriptions et
                  Belles-Lettres*, Paris
CTCA   A. Herdner, *Corpus des Tablettes en Cunéiformes
                  Alphabétiques découvertes à Ras Shamra – Ugarit de
                  1929 à 1939*, Mission de Ras Shamra 10, Paris,
                  1963

EHAT   Exegetisches Handbuch zum Alten Testament,
                  Münster
ET   English translation
EVV   English Versions
ExpT   *The Expository Times*, Edinburgh

GMVO   *Götter und Mythen im Vorderen Orient*, Wörterbuch
                  der Mythologie I.1, ed. H. W. Haussig, Stuttgart,
                  1965

HAT   Handbuch zum Alten Testament, Tübingen
HDB   J. Hastings (ed.), *A Dictionary of the Bible*, Edin-
                  burgh, 1898–1901
HDB[2]   F. C. Grant and H. H. Rowley (eds.), Hastings'
                  Dictionary of the Bible (revised one volume edition),
                  Edinburgh, 1963

HKAT	Handkommentar zum Alten Testament, Göttingen
HTR	*The Harvard Theological Review*, Cambridge (Mass.)
HUCA	*Hebrew Union College Annual*, Cincinnati
IB	*The Interpreter's Bible*, New York – Nashville
ICC	The International Critical Commentary, Edinburgh
IDB	*The Interpreter's Dictionary of the Bible*, New York – Nashville, 1962
IEJ	*Israel Exploration Journal*, Jerusalem
JAOS	*Journal of the American Oriental Society*, New Haven
JBL	*Journal of Biblical Literature*, Philadelphia
JCS	*Journal of Cuneiform Studies*, New Haven
Jer.Bib.	*The Jerusalem Bible*, London, 1966
JNES	*Journal of Near Eastern Studies*, Chicago
JRAS	*Journal of the Royal Asiatic Society of Great Britain and Ireland*, London
JSS	*Journal of Semitic Studies*, Manchester
JTS	*Journal of Theological Studies*, Oxford
KAI	H. Donner and W. Röllig, *Kanaanäische und Aramäische Inschriften*, Wiesbaden, 1962–4
KAT	Kommentar zum Alten Testament, Leipzig – Gütersloh
K-B	L. Koehler and W. Baumgartner, *Lexicon in Veteris Testamenti Libros*, Leiden, 1958
KHC	Kurzer Hand-Commentar zum Alten Testament, (Freiburg, Leipzig), Tübingen
LXX	Septuagint
MS(S)	Manuscript(s)
MT	Massoretic Text
NCB	The New Clarendon Bible, Oxford
NEB	*The New English Bible*, Oxford and Cambridge, 1970
NF	Neue Folge

NS   New Series

OTL   The Old Testament Library, London
OTS   Oudtestamentische Studiën, Leiden

Pauly-Wissowa   G. Wissowa (ed.), *Paulys Real-Encyclopädie der classischen Altertumswissenschaft*, Stuttgart, 1894ff.
PEFQS   *Palestine Exploration Fund Quarterly Statement*, London
Pesh   Peshitta
PEQ   *Palestine Exploration Quarterly*, London

RA   E. Ebeling and B. Meissner (eds.), *Reallexikon der Assyriologie*, Berlin and Leipzig, 1932ff.
RB   *Revue Biblique*, Paris
RHR   *Revue de l'Histoire des Religions*, Paris
RSV   The Revised Standard Version of the Bible, 1952
RV   The Revised Version of the Bible, 1885

SBT   Studies in Biblical Theology, London
SJT   *Scottish Journal of Theology*, Edinburgh
SO   Studia Orientalia edidit Societas Orientalis Fennica, Helsinki
SVT   Supplements to *Vetus Testamentum*, Leiden

TGUOS   *Transactions of the Glasgow University Oriental Society*, Glasgow

UT   C. H. Gordon, *Ugaritic Textbook*, AnOr 38, Rome, 1965

VAB   Vorderasiatische Bibliothek, Leipzig
Vg   Vulgate
VT   *Vetus Testamentum*, Leiden

WC   Westminster Commentaries, London

ZA   *Zeitschrift für Assyriologie und verwandte Gebiete*, Leipzig, Berlin
ZAW   *Zeitschrift für die alttestamentliche Wissenschaft*, Giessen, Berlin
ZDMG   *Zeitschrift der Deutschen Morgenländischen Gesellschaft*, Leipzig
ZThK   *Zeitschrift für Theologie und Kirche*, Tübingen

I

INTRODUCTION

When Ahaz, King of Judah, went to Damascus in 732 BC to meet Tiglath-pileser III, he became an Assyrian vassal and the status of his nation was to remain more or less unchanged for over a hundred years. This century is noted in the book of Kings (II Kings 16—23) as one of the most corrupt in the history of Israel's religion, and many scholars during the past fifty years have argued or assumed that the religious decadence of the age resulted mainly from the Assyrians' policy of imposing the worship of their gods on subject peoples. The decline began, it is believed, when Ahaz set up an altar, usually said to be Assyrian, in the Temple. Then, after an unsuccessful attempt to cast off the Assyrian yoke in the reign of Hezekiah, the situation deteriorated rapidly during the seventh century BC under Manasseh. Throughout this period, it is maintained, the presence of Assyrian cults encouraged the revival of other pagan practices which rapidly multiplied until true Yahwism was almost completely swamped in a morass of heathenism. In 622 BC Josiah, in an act of rebellion against his overlord, cast out the Assyrian gods from the Temple and the land, together with the other foreign cults, and asserted his independence by re-establishing the sole cult of Yahweh as the national god of Judah.

This interpretation of history was brought to the attention of Old Testament scholarship in 1923 by Theodor Östreicher[1] and has since become more or less definitive. Östreicher's arguments may be summarized briefly as follows. Politics and religion in the ancient world cannot be separated from each other; any religious event must also be political. The account of Judah's religion, as

recorded in II Kings 16—23, should therefore be read in the context of world history.[2] Since this was the age of Assyrian suzerainty,
the cult in Jerusalem itself became to all intents and purposes
Assyrian during the reign of Ahaz, who set aside the old altar of
Yahweh and replaced it by a new one dedicated to Ashur of
Nineveh.[3] After the abortive revolt of Hezekiah, Judah remained
faithful to Assyria until, on the occasion of the death of Ashurbanipal (according to Östreicher's chronology in 627 BC, the twelfth
year of Josiah's reign), the Judaean king rose in rebellion and
began his purge of Assyrian gods. In 621 BC further disturbances
in Nineveh afforded an opportunity to continue the purge throughout his kingdom.[4] It was during this year that the finding of the
law-book (II Kings 22) gave additional impetus to the reforms, but
its significance was only incidental,[5] for the basic motivation of the
reformation was political. By the time of Josiah many Assyrian
gods were venerated in the Temple, but the reformers took care
not to arouse the wrath of Assyria by hasty action. Thus the
pagan deities were removed slowly and cautiously, proceeding
from the least important politically to the cult of Ashur itself.[6] At
first only the cultic vessels were taken away (II Kings 23.4),[7] then
the astral cults with their Assyrian priesthood were abolished
(v. 5).[8] With the removal of the cult of Ishtar (vv. 6–7) the old
Solomonic Temple was cleared of Assyrian gods.[9] In preparation
for possible reprisals Josiah desecrated the local sanctuaries in
Judah and around Jerusalem (vv. 8–10) and brought their priests
into the city, lest an Assyrian army should use these cult centres to
gain control over the god of the land and persuade him to fight
against Judah.[10] The climax of the rebellion followed with the
removal of the cult of Shamash (= Ashur), who had his own
sacred buildings in the Temple court (v. 11).[11] Finally, the purges
were completed by the abolition of the few altars left in the
Temple (v. 12) and the desecration of the last remaining cult
centres in the land (vv. 13–14).[12] Josiah had now, by his eighteenth
year, declared his independence from Assyria and had made full
preparations to meet the consequences of his action.

Whilst many of the details of Östreicher's thesis have not
proved acceptable, his central arguments, that Judah was obliged
to accept the cults of her overlord as a sign of vassal status and that
motivation for the reforms of Hezekiah and Josiah was primarily
political, have been widely welcomed and supported.[13] Indeed a

number of scholars have seen in these arguments the solution to the historical and religious problems of the century of Assyrian rule in Judah. For example, Procksch maintained that the account of the reforms in II Kings 23.4–14 can now be understood as a conflation of two sources, one of which (vv. 5, 10–13) records the ejection of Assyrian gods in Josiah's twelfth year, whilst the second (vv. 4, 6–9) describes a purge of Canaanite cults in his eighteenth year.[14] Jepsen, who disagrees with Procksch's analysis, argues from similar premises that the reforms began with the expulsion of Assyrian and other foreign gods and proceeded to a rehabilitation of the cult of Yahweh.[15] Sellin suggested that the absence of anti-Assyrian preaching in Jer. 1—6 may be seen as a further indication that the prophet's ministry began after 628 BC when the overlord's gods had been expelled, but before 621 BC when the reformation was completed.[16] Cross and Freedman have attempted to restate and reaffirm Östreicher's thesis by arguing that all the dates given in II Chron. 34.3ff., including Josiah's eighth year, correlate exactly with major political upheavals in the Assyrian empire during its years of decline.[17] Gressmann also tried to add weight to Östreicher's arguments by providing evidence from Assyrian records which he believed to support the claim that the Assyrians imposed the worship of their gods on defeated peoples. He further maintained that more than half the account of Josiah's reforms related a purge of Assyrian gods (II Kings 23.4–7, 11–12).[18] Olmstead suggested, not only that Yahweh was displaced by Ashur in the reign of Ahaz, but that the Temple now contained a throne for the divine king and probably also a stele-form representation of the Assyrian monarch.[19] Most of the foreign gods and goddesses worshipped in Judah after 732 BC, particularly the Host of Heaven, and even Baal and Asherah, have from time to time been defined as Assyrian, as also have the various pagan rituals and divinatory practices mentioned in the records of this period.[20] The reigns of Ahaz and Manasseh, because marked by (Assyrian) paganism, have been regarded as times when Assyrian overlordship was passively accepted.[21] Even the book of Deuteronomy has been thought to be, in part at least, the deposit of a movement for national revival and independence calling Israel to holy war against all paganism in the land during the Assyrian era.[22] Thus, over the years there has grown a complete interpretation of Judah's history and religion founded on the premiss that, as a vassal kingdom, she was obliged to worship the gods of her overlord, Assyria.

Not every detail of these arguments in support of or dependent on Östreicher's thesis has been found equally acceptable, but for many the central theme has remained convincing. For example, most scholars today would prefer to allow a wider estimation of the role of Deuteronomy in Josiah's reformation and would argue that the reforms were partly motivated by its demands, but they would also maintain that the earlier stages of reform resulted from the pressure of an anti-Assyrian movement for independence.[23] However, in recent years a number of objections have been raised which, taken together, suggest that the whole hypothesis needs to be re-examined. Firstly, it has been questioned whether the altar that Ahaz installed in the Temple was a copy of an Assyrian rather than a Damascene prototype.[24] It has also been proposed that the note in II Chron. 33.10–13 about Manasseh's summons before the Assyrian king may be historically trustworthy and may indicate that he was not always as passively submissive to his overlord as the proliferation of paganism in his reign is taken to suggest.[25] Again, although a few would still maintain that most of the gods worshipped in Judah at this time were Assyrian, an increasing number of scholars are inclined to identify most of them with local Palestinian deities[26] and it has even been argued that the cult of the Host of Heaven was indigenous rather than Assyrian.[27] Finally, it has recently been noted that the contemporary records of the Assyrians provide no clear evidence that they regularly imposed their gods on subject peoples.[28]

These observations have, for the most part, been made with reference, not to Östreicher's hypothesis as a whole, but to specific details in the Old Testament narratives. Nor have they always constituted invectives against the thesis itself, but are often presented as modifications of it. However, if their presuppositions are correct, together they suggest that the hypothesis itself is beginning to crumble. In view of this, it seems that the time has now come for biblical scholars to look again at the accounts of Judah's relationship with her Assyrian overlord, to test the premisses and arguments of Östreicher and his followers and to re-evaluate the significance of the available sources for our understanding of the nature of Israelite history and religion in this period. It is to this task that the following chapters are addressed.

II

THE REIGN OF AHAZ:
CHANGES IN THE RELIGION OF JUDAH

During the reign of Jotham, Damascus and Israel revolted against Tiglath-pileser III, who had but recently brought these two nations under his sway (II Kings 15.19–20). They formed a defensive alliance against Assyria, but, as they were unable to persuade Jotham to join them, they led their armies against Judah (II Kings 15.37) with the intention of putting a puppet monarch on the Southern throne (Isa. 7.1, 5–6).[1] Such was the crisis that faced Ahaz, Jotham's son, in 734 BC. According to II Kings 16, Ahaz, being hard pressed by the coalition and being troubled at the same time by either Arameans or Edomites in the south, bought the assistance of Tiglath-pileser at considerable cost to the Temple and palace treasuries. The Assyrian king responded immediately and Damascus fell (vv. 5–9). Ahaz then went to Damascus to meet Tiglath-pileser and there saw an altar, the pattern of which he sent to Uriah, the priest in Jerusalem, with instructions that a replica be constructed in the Temple (vv. 10–16). On his return Ahaz removed certain structures from the palace and the Temple 'because of the king of Assyria' (vv. 17–18).

The most widely accepted interpretation of this record in chapter 16 is that Ahaz went to Damascus to offer his submission to Tiglath-pileser and was obliged, as a condition of vassal status,[2] to introduce Assyrian deities to the Temple. This he did by constructing a copy of the Assyrian altar at Damascus, and as a further sign of submission he removed or rearranged some of the Temple structures.[3] However, Ahaz's dealings with Assyria are by no means as clear as the simple account in Kings suggests. The events leading to the fall of Damascus are related as if set in motion

by the initiative of Ahaz himself, but Tiglath-pileser's own record
makes no distinction between Ahaz and some eighteen other kings
of the West who were forced to pay tribute.[4] It is indeed likely that
events would have taken a similar course whether Ahaz had
appealed to Tiglath-pileser or not, for the activities of Samaria
amounted to rebellion against Assyrian overlordship. Thus the
records of Tiglath-pileser and of II Kings 16 may simply portray
complementary aspects of the same picture as viewed by Assyrians
and Judaeans respectively. The impression given by the Chronicler,
therefore, that the initiative lay with Tiglath-pileser who demanded
that Judah pay tribute (II Chron. 28.20–21), cannot be lightly dismissed as a distortion of history. There are further features of
II Chron. 28 which may suggest that the Chronicler was reasonably
well informed about the reign of Ahaz, such as his record of the
uprising of Edom (v. 17),[5] his additional note on the intervention
of Philistia (v. 18)[6] and his extra material concerning the Syro-
Ephraimite War (vv. 5–15).[7] Consequently, even though his
account is overwritten with theological considerations which
dictated a revision of II Kings 16,[8] some of his remaining interpretations may be of value.

One of the Chronicler's elaborations on II Kings 16 is that Ahaz
'sacrificed to the gods of Damascus who had defeated him, and
said, "Because the gods of the kings of Aram helped them, I will
sacrifice to them so that they may help me"' (v. 23). It seems at this
point that the Chronicler is not relying solely on Kings for his
information. His statement is hardly a logical deduction from
II Kings 16.10ff., for there the gods of Damascus were shown by
their defeat to have been ineffectual against the power of Assyria
(II Kings 16.9). Nor does his note as it stands appear to be of great
historical value, since it is most improbable that Ahaz would ever
have worshipped the gods of his defeated foes. On the other hand,
there is good reason to suppose that the Chronicler had a piece of
trustworthy historical information, possibly drawn from priestly
or Temple sources, which he is here interpreting as best he can,
namely that the altar of Ahaz was a copy of the altar of Hadad of
Damascus, not an Assyrian altar. In support of this conclusion it
may be argued that, since Ahaz's new altar was made the centre-
piece of the Temple cultus, it is more likely that it was a copy of
'the great altar in the temple at Damascus than an Assyrian altar
erected by the army of occupation'.[9] Furthermore, the new altar

was used for burnt offerings according to the sacrificial practices of the Jerusalem Temple (II Kings 16.13, 15), but the Assyrians did not have altars for the offering of burnt animal sacrifices. An Assyrian altar would have been for incense, libation or display of offerings.[10] Of course, it could be argued that the Assyrians had set up an elaborate altar in Damascus and not simply a temporary military one and that Ahaz in copying it had altered its shape and size to suit the different practices of the Jerusalem cultus,[11] but these are somewhat tortuous arguments and the weight of evidence now points to a Syro-Phoenician altar rather than an Assyrian one.

Olmstead, following Östreicher, believed that just as the new altar had replaced the old one in the Temple, so Ashur had replaced Yahweh in the cultus.[12] But it is by no means clear that the introduction of the new altar brought a foreign cult into the Jerusalem Temple. A new official god would have required a new official priest,[13] yet Uriah, the priest of Yahweh, whom Isaiah had previously considered to be a 'trustworthy witness',[14] was put in charge of the service of the new altar (II Kings 16.15). Furthermore, it seems that the new altar stood directly before the Temple of Yahweh[15] and, since it was used in this position by the priest of Yahweh, it is but logical to conclude that the new altar was dedicated to the worship of Yahweh himself. None the less, the altar cannot have been introduced simply for aesthetic reasons.[16] There must have been something non-Yahwistic about this new altar, otherwise it is difficult to understand why the Deuteronomist related its introduction at length. It has been noted that there is no criticism of Ahaz's action in II Kings 16.10–16,[17] but it may also be noted that there is no praise for him either. Since it is the Deuteronomist's intention to portray Ahaz as an apostate (II Kings 16.2–4), the incident must have been included in the history as an example of the evils of his reign. There are, however, two alternative solutions to this problem,[18] each of which takes full account of the information given and avoids the problems associated with the theory that Ahaz was obliged to introduce the worship of Ashur to the Temple. The first is a recent suggestion that the altar from Damascus was introduced to the Temple as part of an attempt to strengthen Judah's trading links with Phoenicia. Archaeology shows that during the final third of the eighth century BC Judaean economy remained stable despite the

tribute paid to Assyria[19] and it is therefore postulated that one of
the reasons why Ahaz approached Tiglath-pileser in the first
instance was to gain concessions which would ensure continued
trade with Tyre. The plan succeeded and consequently Judah was
able to maintain her level of prosperity. On this hypothesis the
new altar was most certainly Syro-Phoenician.[20] Alternatively, it
may still be argued, and with equal if not greater plausibility,[21]
that this altar was introduced under obligation, if it be presup-
posed that it was a copy of the altar on which Ahaz himself had
ratified his treaty with Tiglath-pileser. The treaty with Assyria
would have meant that Yahweh was now the god of a vassal
kingdom and could thus no longer be worshipped on the old altar
which symbolized his own unique supremacy. His altar must now
be appropriate to the new status of the nation which he ruled and
must therefore be related to the treaty in which Ahaz had declared Judah vassal. If this is correct, then the new altar was
doubtless of Syro-Phoenician pattern, for the Assyrians would
most likely have insisted on sacrifices of both kinds for the sealing
of the treaty.[22]

The fate of the old altar is revealed in the king's words in v. 15:
ūmizbaḥ hanneḥōšet yihyeh-lī leḇaqqēr. A variety of interpretations
have been suggested for the *Piʿēl* infinitive, *leḇaqqēr*,[23] but most
scholars see in it a reference to the taking of omens,[24] to the 'in-
trusion of the vast Babylonian system of omen-sacrifices'.[25] The
reading of omens from entrails was not, however, peculiar to
Assyria and may have been practised independently in Judah. At
least the discovery of a few clay livers at archaeological sites suggests that the practice was not unknown in Palestine at an earlier
period.[26] Furthermore, there is no evidence to suggest that an altar
played any part when the Assyrians cut open a sheep to inspect its
liver.[27] On the other hand, it may be that *leḇaqqēr* was a properly
Yahwistic term meaning 'to enquire' in the sense of performing a
cultic act in order to obtain an oracle, for *leḇaqqēr* in the Temple
was something that the pious Yahwist longed to do.[28]

Although it is unfortunately difficult to formulate more exact
conclusions from the above discussion, it now seems fairly clear
that the account in II Kings 16.5–16 can no longer be interpreted
with the confidence that has hitherto been shown in terms of the
imposition of the worship of Ashur on Judah. But scholars have
also appealed to the verses that follow for support for their con-

clusions. For example, Olmstead considered that the destructive measures recorded in v. 17 illustrate the way in which Yahweh was replaced by Ashur in Jerusalem. He argues that, when Ahaz removed the bronze oxen from beneath 'the sea', 'no longer could the oxen . . . suggest the might of Yahweh.'[29] Unfortunately the religious significance of the bulls is unknown,[30] but the most obvious interpretation of this and other details in v. 17 is simply that Ahaz needed the metals to pay the tribute-money.[31] Verse 18 holds even greater obscurities and many textual difficulties. It tells of some kind of structure[32] which stood in the Temple and of a royal entrance[33] which Ahaz turned round towards the Temple (perhaps, in the Temple),[34] or possibly removed altogether *mippᵉnē melek 'aššūr*. In the present discussion the main verb and the closing phrase of this verse are the primary *cruces interpretatum*. Olmstead thought that *mippᵉnē* should be translated 'from before the face of' and interpreted thus: 'the outer royal entry was turned . . . from before the face of the king of Assyria, presumably represented in stele form',[35] but the evidence that Assyrian kings had their statues erected in temples is limited and it seems likely that the practice was confined to Assyrian temples only.[36] There is otherwise nothing in this obscure verse itself to support Olmstead's suggestion. If the structures in question enhanced the independent sovereignty of the Judaean king, it is certainly possible that Tiglath-pileser would have demanded their destruction or modification and there is no reason why the commonly accepted translation 'because of the king of Assyria' should not be correct. On the other hand, many commentators would prefer to see v. 18 more closely associated with v. 17 and hence they emend the verb *hēsēb* (he turned round) to *hēsîr* (he removed), suggesting an action necessitated by the imposition of tribute, on the assumption that the materials used in the constructions were of some monetary value.[37] Whichever reading is accepted, this verse is open to several interpretations, some of which are as adequate as, if not preferable to, that which finds in it support for the hypothesis that Ahaz introduced the worship of Assyrian gods to the Jerusalem Temple as an act of obligation to his new overlord.

Elsewhere mention is made of Ahaz's upper chamber which was furnished with altars on its roof,[38] and it has often been thought that this structure was erected for the worship of astral deities. This suggestion is entirely possible, for the roof-top was particularly suited to worship in the presence of the stars in Mesopotamia[39] and to worship of the Host of Heaven in Palestine (Jer. 19.13; Zeph. 1.5), while the chamber itself was the scene of an extraordinary solar event (II Kings 20.8–11; Isa. 38.7–8). On the other hand, the roof in Syria-Palestine was one of the places where Baal was worshipped (Jer. 32.29). Similarly, Mesha of Moab ascended the city wall to offer the sacrifice of his son, presumably to Kemosh (II Kings 3.27), and Keret 'sacrificed to his father, the Bull El, and presented his sacrifice to Baal' at the top of a tower,[40] probably the tower of the temple of Baal.[41] The Nabataeans also appear to have used the roof-top as a place for erecting altars for the daily offering of libations and incense to the Sun.[42] Ahaz's roof altars were not therefore necessarily dedicated to the worship of astral deities at all. But even if they were, there is nothing to indicate that the deities worshipped there were Assyrian, as several scholars have maintained.[43]

In conclusion, there can be no doubt that both the Deuteronomist and the Chronicler believed that Ahaz's apostasy was mainly to the gods of Canaan. The accusations levelled against Ahaz are that he 'walked in the way of the kings of Israel',[44] 'passed his son through the fire according to the abominable practices of the nations whom Yahweh drove out before the children of Israel',[45] worshipped the Baals and Molech[46] and indulged in the Canaanite fertility rites of the *bāmōt* cults.[47] Josephus certainly had the impression that his apostasy was κατὰ τὰ Χαναναίων ἔθη.[48]

It seems strange that the Deuteronomist, who so clearly enumerated the Assyrian and other gods imported to Israel after 722 BC (II Kings 17.30–1), should not have mentioned Ashur, if his cult was officially introduced to Jerusalem in 732 BC, and his silence suggests that the veneration of Assyrian gods, which, in view of the political situation, must have taken place in Ahaz's reign, was no more official nor any more important as a mark of apostasy than the many Canaanite cults which flourished at that time.[49]

There must, however, be some historical reason for the sudden popularity of so many different pagan practices at this particular time, and it can hardly be doubted that the cause was more than mere accident or coincidence. Such extensive apostasy must somehow be a symptom of the political upheaval of the age. Although it may no longer be possible to determine precisely how each cultic innovation and heathen digression arose, certain general observations may be offered here.

One of the most significant notes in the Old Testament record of this period is that, faced with the Syro-Ephraimite threat, Ahaz's 'heart and the heart of his people shook as the trees of the forest shake before the wind' (Isa. 7.2).[50] The prophet Isaiah, perceiving the danger in this fear which gripped the land, appealed to the king to renew his trust and confidence in the power of Yahweh to save (vv. 4ff.). Ahaz, however, rejected his advice and turned to the Assyrians for help, with the result that Judah lost her independence and was burdened with heavy tribute, to meet the cost of which the Temple was robbed of its wealth. Simultaneously, the ancient altar before the Temple was replaced by one which probably stood as a symbol of Yahweh's degraded status. The God of Israel had been shown to be powerless before his enemies and was now stripped of his glory. Fear and degradation were the marks of the age, and in such times superstitious and pagan rites spring up quickly amongst the people (cf. Isa. 8.19).

> It is only in times of social dissolution, as in the last age of the small Semitic states, when men and their gods were alike powerless before the advance of the Assyrians, that magical superstitions based on mere terror, or rites designed to conciliate alien gods, invade the sphere of tribal or national religion. In better times the religion of the tribe or state has nothing in common with the private and foreign superstitions or magical rites that savage terror may dictate to the individual.[51]

The king's faint-hearted example merely encouraged the religious decline and soon the old heathenism of Canaanite and popular religion was to be seen everywhere in both Temple and land. Quite naturally, as the Assyrian armies advanced and the Northern Kingdom fell, as the people of Judah saw their brethren being carried into captivity, as they heard the strange voices of new settlers on their borders (II Kings 17), the fear in the hearts of Ahaz and his subjects must have increased. Conditions were ideally suited for the rise of superstitious and pagan rites and it would indeed have been most surprising if the reign of Ahaz had not been marked by apostasy. No doubt many turned to the powerful gods of Assyria at this time, but they probably did so in much the same way as they turned to Baal, Molech, the Stars and a host of other heathen deities. The resort to other gods, both foreign and indigenous, was a natural reaction to historical circumstances, not an action dictated by imperial decree. Doubtless there were also many other factors operative in the promotion of religious decadence, but it now seems most unlikely that one of these was an obligation laid on Judah to worship Assyrian gods.

III

HEZEKIAH'S REFORMATION AND REBELLION

It may be argued that if Assyrian gods were no more important than other pagan deities in the reign of Ahaz, they must certainly have been prominent in the reforms of Hezekiah. Rowley believed that 'if no account of any reform had been given we should have been bound to assume that there was one . . . any king who rebelled against Assyria would repudiate the Assyrian deities',[1] and many scholars today would agree with this opinion.[2]

II Kings 18.4 summarizes the record of the reformation in these words:

> He removed the *bāmōt* and broke in pieces the *maṣṣēbōt* and cut up the *'ašērim*[3] and cut in pieces the bronze serpent which Moses made, for until these days the children of Israel were burning sacrifice to it; it was called Nehushtan.

Gray believes that this verse reads like an excerpt from an annalistic source,[4] but others have maintained that only the record of the destruction of Nehushtan is original and that v. 4a is an editorial expansion, possibly in the light of Josiah's reforms.[5] However, the theme of *bāmōt, maṣṣēbōt* and *'ašērim* as the marks of apostasy is central to the Deuteronomist's historical thesis which finds its climax in their removal by the great reformers.[6] According to the Deuteronomist the origins of these aberrations lie in the early days of monarchic history, for even in the days of Rehoboam, he relates, 'they built for themselves *bāmōt* and *maṣṣēbōt* and *'ašērim* on every high hill and under every green tree' (I Kings 14.23). Consequently, it cannot be maintained that v. 4a in any way cloaks a special hidden reference to the removal of Assyrian cults. Likewise, the cult of the bronze serpent is acknowledged to be ancient and the tradition of its Mosaic origin is probably reflected in the wilderness story in Num. 21.6-9. It has been suggested that it was originally a Zadokite cult symbol,[7] or a symbol of healing related to the god Horon,[8] but the serpent is a well known feature in the Canaanite fertility cult, often closely associated with the mother-goddess in Canaanite art.[9] Furthermore, it is now known that the Midianites, with whom Israel is closely associated in the wilderness tradition through the marriage of Moses to Jethro's daughter, venerated a bronze serpent in their shrine at Timna.[10] Hence the tradition of the wilderness origin of Nehushtan is in no way impossible. Nevertheless, it seems fairly clear that Nehushtan also belonged to the cultural context of the indigenous cults.

It is also noteworthy that the Rabshakeh, in urging the people of Jerusalem to submit to Sennacherib, made no mention of Ashur or the Assyrian gods in either of his speeches.[11] In his first speech he mocks Hezekiah's reliance on his own small and impotent army (II Kings 18.23-4) and on Egypt, the 'broken reed', as an ally (v. 21). He also makes fun of the people's reliance on Yahweh whose altars their king has been destroying (v. 22) and whose help the Assyrian himself has enlisted (v. 25). In his second speech he goes on to claim that Yahweh, like the gods of the other nations round about, is impotent to save against the might of Assyria (vv. 32-5). The content of this second oration is most certainly in accord with the common claims of the Assyrians[12] and it seems that Hezekiah was well aware of how history was tending to show that they were not empty claims.[13] It is also possible that the Rabshakeh's taunt in the first speech reveals that Hezekiah had failed in his aim, by bringing his priests into Jerusalem and destroying the local shrines, to prevent the Assyrians from placating Yahweh, the god of the land.[14] But it is surely significant that the Rabshakeh makes no allusion to the removal of Assyrian gods, which, according to some scholars, was Hezekiah's central act of rebellion.

Finally, in II Kings 18.5-8 the editor introduces the history of Sennacherib's campaigns in Judah by describing Hezekiah's faith in Yahweh which led him to 'rebel against the king of Assyria' (v. 7). Sennacherib himself records how Hezekiah withheld tribute and led an alliance of Palestinian states against Assyria,[15] but nowhere in either account is a purge of Assyrian gods mentioned. The consuming interest of the Deuteronomic historian in recounting Hezekiah's reign is the relationship between Palestine and Mesopotamia. It is almost unbelievable that, if the worship of Assyrian gods in the Temple was a central feature in this relationship, the Deuteronomist should have passed over it in silence and have preferred to record such trivialities as the removal of an otherwise unknown bronze serpent,[16] or to summarize the reforms in terms of Canaanite cult symbols. While the restitution of Yahweh's independent sovereignty, which is implied in the Rabshakeh's taunt in II Kings 18.28–35, may have been motivated as much by political as by religious considerations, and while it is likely that the political and religious fervour of rebellion would have ensured the abolition of any Assyrians gods which had found their way into Jerusalem, there is nothing to suggest that Hezekiah's reformation was in any way a rebellious purge of official Assyrian cults. Furthermore, the act of centralization may suggest that there were motives for the reformation far deeper than political aspiration.[17]

II Chron. 29—32, however, presents a very different picture of Hezekiah's reign. Throughout these chapters Hezekiah is depicted as the good and virtuous king who has done everything according to the will of Yahweh and who can have the Assyrian army repulsed by a prophet's prayer. The Chronicler is writing midrash,[18] but his witness to the reformation may not for this reason be dismissed as lacking the evidence of historical records.[19]

II Kings 18.4 finds its parallel in II Chron. 31.1 where the purge of the *bāmōt*, *maṣṣēbōt* and *'ašērīm* is extended to the Northern Kingdom. Since this notice provides no additional information about the nature of the cults in question, it must be interpreted in the same way as II Kings 18.4. On the other hand, the Chronicler does give additional information about the reformation which, it could be argued, lends support to the idea that Hezekiah purged the Temple of official Assyrian religion. II Chron. 29.3–6 describes how Hezekiah opened the doors of the Temple which Ahaz had closed (cf. II Chron. 28.24) and informed the Levites gathered in the eastern square of the Temple how their fathers had 'turned away their faces from the dwelling-place of Yahweh and turned their backs' (v.6). These details may be 'largely, if not entirely, imaginary'[20] and the Chronicler may have accentuated the apostasy of Ahaz as a foil to the faith of Hezekiah, but it is also possible that vv.3–6 are based in history. According to II Kings 18.16,

Hezekiah had overlaid the door-posts of the Temple, but was compelled to strip them again to pay the tribute to Sennacherib. Hezekiah may have covered the door-posts in the first instance because Ahaz had earlier stripped them to pay the Assyrian tribute, but the Chronicler claims that the doors were closed, and it has been suggested that the Temple doors were officially opened in the pre-exilic period only during the autumn festival.[21] Furthermore, turning the face from the Temple towards the east (v. 6) was part of the ritual of Sun-worship described in Ezek. 8.16 (cf. 11.1?). It could therefore be suggested[22] that Ahaz had ceased to celebrate Yahweh's New Year Festival and had turned to the worship of Ashur whom he regarded as a solar deity. There are, however, several difficulties in this suggestion. It is not at all clear that the language of II Chron. 29.6 does indicate a Sun-cult ritual and is not simply metaphorical of the rejection of Yahwism in a more general way. But if the Chronicler is describing a solar ritual similar to that condemned in Ezekiel, then it is more likely that his material is based on objection to a type of cultic aberration found nearer to his own time than that he has used historical sources dating from Hezekiah's reign. The ritual described in Ezek. 8.16 belongs to period nearer to the exile and apparently continued to be a problem in the post-exilic period, since the Mishnah also abominates prostration to the rising Sun with back turned to the Temple.[23] However, it is unlikely, even if the rite is earlier, that it results from Assyrian influence. Amongst the Assyrians the worship of Shamash would normally have been conducted inside the temple where it was believed that the god lived surrounded by his family and courtiers, for the Assyrians and Babylonians had personified their Sun-god and had come to regard the solar disc as his symbol rather than as the god himself.[24] Perhaps the closest affinities with the kind of Sun-worship ascribed to Hezekiah's subjects is to be found amongst the Syro-Phoenicians.[25] Be that as it may, there is plenty of evidence for solar religion in Palestine from a much earlier date than the Assyrian period[26] and, in addition to this, Ashur's primary nature was not that of Sun-god, but of war-lord. Shamash was the Sun-god of Assyria, and it is doubtful whether Ashur ever was a solar deity, except in as far as he, as chief god of the Assyrian pantheon, was able to assimilate the attributes of Shamash, as of any other deity in the pantheon.[27]

Thus it would seem that the evidence of the Chronicler, like that of the Deuteronomist, lends no support to the thesis that Hezekiah's reformation was motivated by a political desire to rid the land of regnant Assyrian deities. Alternative motivation is, however, not difficult to find.

Though few details of Hezekiah's reformation are known, the summary statement of its content in II Kings 18.4 seems to be of good historical value, as the Rabshakeh's speech[28] and the notice that Hezekiah restored the Temple gates[29] both attest, while the recent excavations of the Yahweh temple at *Tell Arad* show that the altar there was in all likelihood removed in Hezekiah's time.[30] The purge of the *bāmōt* may also have extended into the Northern Kingdom.[31] The note in II Chron. 30.1–12, that the king invited the Israelites to join in his Passover celebrations, carries overtones of the Chronicler's own concern to include the Israelites in the Jerusalem cult activities,[32] but it is possible, even if the account of the Passover is unhistorical,[33] that Hezekiah did show an interest in the Israelites.[34] Indeed, Bethel and Gibeah may both at some time have been under his jurisdiction.[35] Thus there is no reason to doubt that the Deuteronomist is correct in his judgment that the reforms accord with the principles of Deuteronomism. Unfortunately too little is known to warrant a positive statement that the reforms resulted from Deuteronomic pressure, but such a conclusion must remain a valid possibility.

Whilst one of the interpretations most widely accepted today is that Deuteronomy 'emanated from a small group of reformers who wished to embody the lessons of Hezekiah's reforms in a plan for the next occasion that should offer',[36] it may also be argued that the reforming influence on Hezekiah himself was more religious than political, and possibly even Deuteronomic. The prose editor of Jeremiah was certainly of the opinion that the prophet Micah exerted considerable influence on Hezekiah (Jer. 26.18–19) and the word of Isaiah seems to have been particularly authoritative in the royal court (II Kings 19—20; Isa. 37—38). It has also been widely accepted that the early Deuteronomists came to Judah from Israel after the fall of Samaria in 722 BC[37] and there must have been many faithful Yahwists in the South, standing in the ancient traditions of Israel, to whom the Deuteronomic message would have been acceptable. We hear of such ardent Yahwistic groups as the Nazirites (Amos 2.11–12) and the Rechabites (Jer. 35), both highly commended by the prophets. The *'am-hā'āreṣ*, as the part they played at the enthronement of Jehoash reveals (II Kings 11), were also people amongst whom militant anti-paganism had survived the syncretistic policies of several monarchs.[38] The royal cult in Jerusalem may not have welcomed the early Deuteronomists, especially in the reign of Ahaz,[39] but there can be little doubt that there were those in Judah who viewed the syncretism in the Temple at Jerusalem with disgust and who would have welcomed in their midst the true Yahwists of the North. Living with an urgent message authenticated by the catastrophe of 722 BC, their impact on Judaean thought must have been considerable. Hence it is likely that, when Hezekiah came to the throne in 715 BC,[40] the movement had gained sufficient authority to influence the king and his court to some extent. Thus it is not improbable that the religious demands of Deuteronomism in some way were amongst the causes of Hezekiah's reformation, even if several other features influenced the act of centralization itself.[41]

Finally, Noth argues that Hezekiah, after his rebellion, when he submitted once more to Sennacherib,[42] had to make room for the official Assyrian state religion in the royal sanctuary in Jerusalem again, but the evidence of the Old Testament is entirely to the contrary.[43] The unqualified praise of Hezekiah for his trust in Yahweh is unwarranted if he reverted to the worship of Assyrian gods. Isaiah condemned his political diplomacy,[44] but made no mention of desertion to the worship of Assyrian gods. Furthermore, if Jerusalem did experience some kind of miraculous deliverance,[45] it is most unlikely that Hezekiah would subsequently have reintroduced any Assyrian cult. On the other hand, it is equally difficult to believe that when he offered his submission to Sennacherib he simultaneously intended to continue his rebellion by refusing to worship the gods of Assyria. The most logical conclusion from the extant records is therefore that the Assyrians did not at this time impose religious sanctions of the kind Noth supposes. Hezekiah's act of rebellion no doubt involved a declaration of Yahweh's independent sovereignty and probably the destruction of the symbols of his vassal status, such as treaty-documents and perhaps Ahaz's altar, but there is nothing in the records of this period to indicate that he inherited officially imposed Assyrian cults from his father or that such cults were the object of his purge. Whilst it can hardly be doubted that in this age of Assyrian influence there must have been some Assyrian gods in the land of

Judah and that such gods would have been expelled by Hezekiah as part of his reforming policy, there is no reason to assume that these gods had an official status different from that of any other pagan gods in the land.[46]

Any assessment of the age of Hezekiah must include an evaluation of the influence of the prophetic teaching on the king and a recognition of the possibility that there already existed in the land a growing movement for religious reform which was supported by the forebears of the Deuteronomists of Josiah's reign. On the other hand, it can hardly have been mere chance that enabled the king to set his reforms in motion at this particular time when he was also taking steps to cast off the Assyrian yoke. Just as the rise of paganism in the reign of Ahaz was seen to be a symptom of the age, so also its rejection was indubitably closely allied to the spirit of hope which arose in Judah at the end of the eighth century. Hezekiah's alliance with the rebel states of Palestine must have engendered considerable nationalistic zeal in the land and this was probably sufficient to rally the people to the banner of Yahweh. Certainly we find that confidence in Yahweh was restored to the degree that the people were more or less solidly behind the king in his reinstatement of the God of Israel as the only god with the power to save (II Kings 18.5–7, 22, 32, 35). With such a spirit abroad in the land, it is but natural to find that the cult was purged, strengthened and unified and that Yahweh was declared the one and only sovereign god, fully independent and all-powerful. The reformation was therefore not a declaration of rebellion, but one manifestation of the spirit that led to rebellion.

IV

THE 'DARK AGE' OF MANASSEH AND AMON

Since there is little in II Kings 21.1–18 which does not derive from the pen of the Deuteronomist or of the exilic redactor,[1] and since these verses were probably written 'as a prelude to . . . the reformation of Josiah',[2] care must be exercised in distinguishing history from polemic. *Prima facie* there is no reason to doubt that Manasseh did have official Assyrian cults in the Temple. The bald statements that he 'worshipped all the Host of Heaven and served them' (v. 3) and that he 'built altars for all the Host of Heaven in the two courts of the House of Yahweh' (v. 5), although they provide no clue to the nature and provenance of the cult of the Host of Heaven, could, it must be admitted, indicate the presence of Assyrian astral worship. On the other hand, the cult of the Host of Heaven could equally well be indigenous.[3] Likewise, the statement that 'he practised soothsaying and augury, and dealt with mediums and wizards' (v. 6) may be interpreted either way.[4] Furthermore, there is nothing in the text to indicate whether these abuses had been introduced under compulsion or had arisen spontaneously. Nevertheless, the sources at our disposal do give much information about Manasseh's apostasy and they seem to indicate that his official policy may not have been simply Assyrianization.

For the most part the evidence suggests that it was the Canaanite cults that flourished in Judah under Manasseh's patronage. In II Kings 21.2–7 and II Chron. 33.2–7 the king is condemned for his apostasy to 'the abominations of the nations whom Yahweh drove out before the people of Israel'.[5] The *bāmōt* 'which Hezekiah his father had destroyed' were restored, presumably permitting the revival of Canaanite fertility religion.[6] II Kings 21.6 relates how Manasseh 'passed his son through the fire', possibly as a rite in honour of Molech in the Valley of Ben-Hinnom.[7] The note in II Kings 21.3 that 'he erected altars for Baal and made an Asherah' also suggests apostasy to Canaanite gods, or, if 'as Ahab, king of Israel, had done' is an accurate historical comment and not just polemical, apostasy to the gods of Phoenicia.[8] Reference is also made in II Kings 21.7 to a graven image of Asherah which Manasseh erected in the Temple. Whilst it has been argued that this was an image of the Assyrian goddess, Ishtar,[9] there are good reasons for believing that its presence in the Temple is much more a mark of Canaanite, or more properly Phoenician, rather than Assyrian influence.[10]

Thus it would seem that Manasseh's reign saw the general resurgence of the old Canaanite cults which the prophets had condemned in the eighth century BC.[11] But there are hints that Manasseh's apostasy was also deliberate and particular. The mention of Ahab has suggested the possibility of Phoenician gods in Jerusalem. Certain further considerations render this suggestion not improbable. Solomon's pact with Hiram of Tyre and his foreign marriages had resulted in the early presence of Phoenician religion in Jerusalem, which apparently continued until the days of Josiah.[12] Phoenician influence had been renewed in Jerusalem through the marriage of Jehoram to Athaliah, the daughter of Ahab, who reigned as queen over Judah after the death of her husband and encouraged pagan religion in the city.[13] Hence it is by no means unlikely that the building of altars to Baal and the erection of an image of Asherah in the Temple did follow the precedent set by Ahab in the North, as the Deuteronomist suggests. In a recent study Patai has shown that the cult of the Phoenician Asherah was firmly entrenched in Northern Israel from a very early date.[14] As a result of Ahab's marriage with the Sidonian Jezebel a temple was built for Baal in Samaria and an Asherah image was erected (I Kings 16.32–3), whilst the Asherah cult had the support of at least four hundred royal prophets (I Kings 18.19). The Asherah continued to stand in Samaria throughout the ninth century (II Kings 13.6) and appears to have remained until the fall of the kingdom in 722 BC (II Kings 17.16–17). By contrast little is heard of an Asherah image in Jerusalem until the Assyrian period. Maacah's abortive attempt to

introduce an Asherah cult was quickly ended by Asa (I Kings
15.13) and it is not until the time of Manasseh that an Asherah
image is erected again in the Temple.[15] Although there are doubtless many *lacunae* in our knowledge of the history of the Asherah
cult in Israel and Judah,[16] the information given by the Deuteronomist in his history certainly appears to suggest that both the
Baal altars and the Asherah image introduced by Manasseh were
dedicated to Phoenician deities. One further consideration of
detail adds support to this conclusion.

In II Kings 21.7 we find mention of Manasseh's *pesel hā'ăšērā*,
but II Chron. 33.7 changes the text to read *pesel hassemel*. The phrase
in Kings is unique in the Old Testament,[17] for the Asherah is
never described as a *pesel*, and wherever *'ăšērā* and *pesel* appear together in lists of idols, they are always distinguished as different.[18]
There may therefore be good reason why the Chronicler altered
the text of Kings, especially since the word he substituted, *semel*,
is not a common one in the Old Testament (II Chron. 33.7, 15;
Deut. 4.16; Ezek. 8.3, 5 only) and its precise meaning is far from
certain.[19] In addition to a number of unsatisfactory attempts made
by different scholars to establish an Accadian derivation,[20] Albright has suggested that it be related to the Accadian *simmiltu*
(step, stairway) and proposes the meaning 'slab-image'. This
leads him to conclude that the *semel* could not have been of
Phoenician origin,[21] but his conclusion seems most unfortunate,
for the word is found outside the Old Testament only in Phoenician and Punic inscriptions. It would therefore seem more probable that the word *semel* entered the Hebrew language through
the Phoenician. From the Phoenician inscriptions it appears that a
semel was an anthropomorphic idol. It could be dedicated to gods
and goddesses,[22] or could be erected to the memory of the dead,[23]
and it was at least sometimes cast in bronze.[24] Likewise, in the Old
Testament Deut. 4.16 illustrates the *semel* as something that could
be made in the shape of a man or an animal, and most scholars,
though not all, seem to agree that the *semel* in Ezekiel's vision was
anthropomorphic.[25] But whatever the precise significance of the
word, Ezekiel and the Chronicler both agree that there was some
kind of idol in the pre-exilic Temple which could be called a
semel. Since the word is found only in Phoenician and Punic and
since it appears on an inscription as early as the eighth century,[26]
it seems most likely that it was taken into Hebrew, not from an

Accadian word which bears little similarity in its original meaning, but from Phoenician, perhaps in the seventh century BC.[27] Indeed, it is possible that the Chronicler referred to Manesseh's idol as a *semel* precisely because it represented some imported Phoenician goddess, who may have been Astarte,[28] but was more probably Asherah, as is suggested by the Deuteronomist's comparison of Ahaz's apostasy with that of Ahab who had erected an image to the Phoenician Asherah in the ninth century in Samaria. If these suggestions are correct, then it is possible that the peculiar conjunction of the words *pesel* and *ʾašērā* in II Kings 21.7 may be explained on the grounds that there were some marked differences in appearance between this image and the more usual Judaean mother-goddess symbol which is also known as an *ʾašērā* in the Old Testament.

It may now be concluded that Manasseh probably did follow Ahab's example in erecting an image for Asherah, particularly since her cult, it seems, had not hitherto flourished in Judah. It would be reading too much out of this information to add the further conclusion that Manasseh's Asherah cult, like Ahab's, was introduced as a consequence of a diplomatic marriage, but my own suspicion is that such might well have been the case. Nevertheless, there are much stronger grounds for believing that it was precisely because of Manasseh's marriage that Arabian astral religion received royal patronage in Jerusalem.

Links with Arabia are perhaps more tenuous than those with the Syro-Phoenician states, but the visit of a Sabaean queen to the Solomonic court[29] and the discovery of a South Arabian trader's seal at Bethel[30] may place intercourse between pre-exilic Palestine and South Arabia above the level of mere speculation.[31] It is also known that Sargon resettled desert Arabs in Samaria in 715 BC,[32] and in an age of unrest amongst the Arabs of the empire[33] it is possible that some Arabian states corresponded with Judah, just as Babylon had done in the reign of Hezekiah.[34] This conjecture finds some support in the consideration of two significant omissions in the Chronicler's copying of the introduction and conclusion to the reigns of Manasseh and Amon.

The names of Hephzibah and Meshullemeth, the mothers of Manasseh and Amon, are omitted in the Chronicler's history,[35] although he faithfully recorded the name of every preceding Judaean queen-mother where that name was in the Kings parallel.

There is, however, one important and instructive exception. The name of Maacah, the mother of Asa, is omitted in II Chron. 14.1.,[36] although she is inevitably mentioned in the account of her downfall (II Chron. 15.16). The Chronicler, clearly ashamed to claim Maacah as queen-mother of the good King Asa, avoided mentioning her name as far as possible and, when she was introduced as queen-mother of Abijah, he altered her non-Yahwistic name, Maacah daughter of Abishalom, to the more acceptable Micaiah daughter of Uriel (II Chron. 13.2).[37] The name of Hephzibah must similarly have been considered a stain on the reputation of both Manasseh and the Davidic dynasty, as also were the names of the mothers of Amon and Josiah.[38]

Nothing is known about Manasseh's mother except that her name was Hephzibah, but more may be said about the mother of Amon, *Mᵉšullemet bat-Ḥārūṣ* of *Yoṭbā*. Firstly, *Yoṭbā* was two stages from Eziongeber in the account of the wilderness wanderings[39] and is probably to be identified with *aṭ-Ṭaba*, about twenty miles north of Aqaba.[40] This immediately suggests Edomite or Arabian affinities, as also do the names *Ḥārūṣ* and *Mᵉšullemet*. Firstly, *Ḥārūṣ* appears as an Arabian name in inscriptions from Sinai and Lihyani in the form *ḥrwṣw*.[41] Secondly, the name *Mᵉšullemet* is formed from the root *šlm* which was very popular in the formation of male and female names alike in both North and South Arabia.[42] It is therefore probable that the mother of Amon and wife of Manasseh was an Arabian woman, which, presumably, was one good reason why the Chronicler should have excluded her name from his history.

But there appears to have been a more powerful reason for the Chronicler's omission than the mere consideration of ancestry. Contrary to his customary practice of giving accurate records of royal burials,[43] the Chronicler chooses to avoid all reference to the location of Manasseh's grave 'in the Garden of Uzza' and to omit completely the notice that Amon was buried in the same Garden.[44] It has been suggested that the word Uzza (*'uzzā'*) is an abbreviation of King Uzziah's name (*'uzziyyāhū*),[45] but this equation has never proved fully acceptable[46] and the alternative suggestion, that Uzza is the name of the Arabian astral god *Al-'Uzzā*, has won some approval.[47] Since Manasseh's wife was in all probability Arabian, it is not unlikely that some plot of land in Jerusalem had been dedicated to one of her gods, for in ancient Israel marriage to a foreign wife usually resulted in the introduction of the wife's religion.[48]

From our study of the records of Manasseh's reign it may now be concluded that the king permitted or encouraged the general revival of Canaanite religion in Judah and also in particular introduced to Jerusalem the cults of the Sidonian Baal and Asherah and of the Arabian *Al-'Uzzā*. It also appears that these new religions entered the city as a result, at least in one instance, of marriages arranged by Manasseh. On the basis of this information, it is possible to give an interpretation of Judaean history which does not necessitate acceptance of the hypothesis that Manasseh was obliged to maintain Assyrian cults in the Temple and which explains some of the hitherto enigmatic features of the records of his reign.

Assyrian annals include Manasseh in lists of twenty-two kings of Hatti who forwarded building materials to Esarhaddon[49] and who assisted Ashurbanipal in his campaigns against Egypt.[50] These records, together with the total condemnation by the Deuteronomist, are generally taken to indicate that Manasseh was a loyal vassal of Assyria. Nevertheless, it has often been suspected that the account in II Chron. 33.10–13 of his abduction to Babylon may have a historical basis,[51] and it may be that he showed no more fidelity to Assyria than necessity dictated.

At the beginning of Manasseh's reign Assyria was at the peak of her power and even Egypt had been brought under her sway. But the seeds of rebellion were never removed. Babylon was ruled by Shamash-shum-ukin, the elder brother of Ashurbanipal, but unrest continued as usual in both Babylon and Elam. In Egypt Psammetichus I was expanding his power, having the sympathy of Gyges of Lydia who longed for the humiliation of Assyria. Meanwhile, pressure from the Medes on the northern frontier of the empire kept the Assyrians fully occupied and offered Psammetichus an opportunity to withhold tribute, which he probably did in 655 BC or soon after. There seem to have been no repercussions, and Psammetichus and Gyges may have encouraged discontent in Syria-Palestine. When Babylon and Elam rebelled under Shamash-shum-ukin in 652 BC, disaffection spread in Syria-Palestine and at the same time desert Arabs overran the Assyrian vassal states in Edom, Moab and other lands in eastern Palestine and Syria. Although it is not known whether Judah was actively

involved in the rebellions, the close relations which, if the foregoing arguments are correct, existed between her and some of the
Arabian and Phoenician states could have induced Manasseh at
least to express his sympathy with the rebel cause. However, the
revolts could not be sustained. In 648 BC Babylon was crushed and
Elam suffered a similar fate some years later. Ashurbanipal also
turned to the west where he conducted lengthy campaigns against
the Arabs. Egypt was never reconquered, but Palestine may have
been subdued and resettled at this time.[52] At some stage during
these disturbances, probably soon after 648 BC,[53] Manasseh, because of his friendships with the Arabs and the Phoenicians, may
have been taken to Babylon and required to reaffirm his allegiance. Subsequently he may have been allowed or commissioned
to fortify Jerusalem and to garrison the cities of his land with his
own army so that Judah could become a buffer-state against
Egypt.[54] Amon, his son and successor, continued to accept passively the overlordship of Assyria, and it was perhaps for this
reason that, after only two years on the throne, he was assassinated
by members of an anti-Assyrian[55] or a pro-Egyptian party.[56]

The Deuteronomist gave no details of Manasseh's reign, but
was solely concerned to depict his age as Israel's darkest as a foil
to the reign of Josiah. Doubtless the Chronicler also exaggerated
the comprehensiveness of Manasseh's reforms, but there is reason
to believe that underlying his account is an element of truth.
Manasseh probably sympathized with his neighbours in their
rebellion, being united to them by marriages and other now unknown ties. These unions have left their traces on the accounts of
the reign, indicating also that Manasseh was apostate to the
paganism of Canaan, Phoenicia, Arabia and possibly even Egypt.[57]
If these suggestions are correct, the field from which the deities
compounding the Host of Heaven in Manasseh's reign could have
been drawn is much extended, since astral religion was not alien to
Arabia and Phoenicia.[58] It is therefore not at all obvious that the
mere mention of the Host of Heaven in II Kings 21 can be regarded as indicative of the presence of enforced Assyrian cults
(never mentioned otherwise) in the Jerusalem Temple.[59]

In the final analysis it must be recognized that, just as the actions
of both Ahaz and Hezekiah were governed largely by the age in
which they lived, so also the reign of Manasseh was ideally suited
to the revival of paganism. As the Assyrians asserted their author-

ity, Judah began to recognize her weakness and the excitement of rebellion died. No doubt, when the people realized that there was no real hope of independence in the foreseeable future, their religious fervour was also quenched. Disillusioned once more by the ineffectuality of their national god, many must have turned to the stronger gods of Assyria and to the cults which offered more immediate satisfaction. The old Canaanite cults reappeared and their local sanctuaries were restored throughout the country, including the savage rites of the Hinnom Valley. The religions of popular superstition flourished again and soon star-worship,[60] soothsaying, augury, necromancy and wizardry became common in both city and land. It does, however, also seem fairly clear that Manasseh himself positively encouraged this revival of heathenism, since he introduced the gods of his intimate allies, permitted both foreign and superstitious religion in the Temple precincts, and attempted to silence opposition. He is therefore rightly condemned by the Deuteronomist, but one wonders how it could have been otherwise, for this was an age when the voice of Yahwism was inevitably falling on deaf ears.

V

THE REFORMS OF JOSIAH

Here we reach the crucial point of our discussion, for it was in the context of the study of Josiah's reforms that Östreicher proposed his reinterpretation of Judah's history. He saw Josiah's action not so much in terms of a religious reformation as in terms of a political revolt against Assyrian suzerainty, and in this context the iconoclasm became an outward expression of rebellion in the form of a public rejection of the gods which had been the official symbols of vassal status. Whilst many have accepted Östreicher's hypothesis without critical analysis of its presuppositions, a few have attempted to give it added weight by adducing further supporting evidence.[1] However, one of the main difficulties with Östreicher's interpretation is that it leaves little or no room for the influence of the law-book, usually thought to be *Urdeuteronomium*, which was presented to Josiah in the eighteenth year of his reign, 622 BC.[2] Indeed, Östreicher himself admitted that 'the finding of the law-book . . . had not really the decisive significance which is ascribed to it today',[3] but most present-day scholars, it seems, would prefer some modified version of his thesis. It would now be generally acknowledged that the reforms of 622 BC were primarily motivated by the demands of *Urdeuteronomium*, but it would be argued that there had been an earlier phase of reform, as the Chronicler suggests, which was entirely independent of the book and resulted from the pressure of 'a movement towards independence and national self-assertion'.[4]

However, it is not at all clear that the extant texts do suggest a purge of Assyrian gods, as Östreicher and his supporters have supposed. There appear to have been three main aspects to

Josiah's reforms as described in II Kings 23.4–20, 24: the purge of the Temple and its precincts, the destruction of the *bāmōt* in Jerusalem and Judah, and the desecration of the sanctuaries of the old Northern Kingdom. Such a threefold division is supported by the Chronicler, but he gives little information about the gods expelled that is of any value in the present study. The purge of the Temple is ascribed to Manasseh who, it is said (II Chron. 33.15–16):

> took away the foreign gods and the *semel* from the House of Yahweh, and all the altars that he had built on the mountain of the House of Yahweh and in Jerusalem, and he threw them outside the city. He restored the altar of Yahweh . . .

The Chronicler has manifestly summarized and presented a generalized account of the reforms. Similar generalized expression is found in the account he gives of Josiah's purge of the *bāmōt* (II Chron. 34.3–5):

> he began to purge Judah and Jerusalem of the *bāmōt*, the *'ašērīm*, the *pesīlīm* and the *massēkōt*. And they broke down the altars of the *be'altīm* in his presence; and he hewed down the *ḥammānīm* which were above them; and he broke in pieces the *'ašērīm*, the *pesīlīm* and the *massēkōt* and made dust of them and scattered it over the graves of those who sacrificed to them. He also burned the bones of the priests on their altars and purged Judah and Jerusalem.

II Chron. 34.6–7 describes the purge of the Northern Kingdom in almost identical terms: altars and *ḥammānīm* (which used to be regarded as Sun-pillars, but are now more commonly thought to be incense-altars) were cut down and *'ašērīm* and *pesīlīm* were ground to dust. Clearly the Chronicler is outlining the accounts of the reformation in a summary fashion and the repetitive use of formulae prohibits close analysis of the nature of the cults in question. Nevertheless, although it is probably of significance, as Östreicher suggested, that the Chronicler has protracted the reformation over a fairly long period and that mostly before the production of the law-book, it is hardly legitimate to argue from his account in II Chron. 33—34 that the first stage of the reforms was anti-Assyrian, for the Chronicler's division is geographical, indicating that the purge of the Temple, not a purge of Assyrian gods, came first and that the purge of the *bāmōt* followed.

Therefore, if II Kings 23.4–14 does combine two sources, as many scholars have maintained, and the Chronicler knew that this was the case, it seems most likely that one dealt with the purge of the Temple and the other with the desecration of the *bāmōt*.[5] Now it would be expected that official Assyrian cults would be most strongly represented in the Temple and that their presence there would have secondarily influenced the practices of the *bāmōt*. We shall therefore consider the Temple reforms first, following the account as it is contained in II Kings 23.4, 6–7, 11–12.

Gressmann argued that Baal, Asherah and all the Host of Heaven in v. 4 were in reality Assyrian gods and he referred to Ashurbanipal's requirement that the Babylonians give offerings for Ashur, Ninlil[6] and all the gods of Assyria. But this suggestion has not found general approval, because, as Montgomery correctly remarked, the terminology here is Syro-Palestinian.[7] Baal and Asherah were Canaanite deities whose roles in religion and mythology are now well known from the Ras Shamra texts. Although Asherah is not Baal's consort in the Ugaritic myths, the two commonly appear together in the Old Testament as the rivals of Yahweh and there is no reason to suppose that their names in this instance conceal a reference to Assyrian gods. Although no exact parallel to the phrase 'Baal, Asherah and all the Host of Heaven' has been found, the Zakir inscription from Afis makes mention of 'Baalshamem . . . and Shamash and Sahr and . . . the gods of heaven and the gods of earth',[8] and 'the great Baal, Moon and Sun' appear on an inscription from Tarsus.[9] These Syrian texts at least show that the gods of heaven were associated with Baal in some of his manifestations in the eighth century, before the time of Assyrian conquest. This is particularly relevant, if, as has been argued, the Baal and Asherah cult of Manasseh was of Phoenician origin, for it would then be most likely that the Host of Heaven referred to here derived from a similar background. Anyhow, since the terminology is Syro-Palestinian, the probability is that the deities are also Syro-Palestinian.[10] This conclusion from the use of terminology must not, however, be left without qualification, for it was fairly common in the ancient world for foreign gods to be equated with indigenous deities and to adopt their names. For example, Bar-rekub of Zinjirli in the eighth century BC referred to the Mesopotamian Moon-god, Sin, as *b'l* of Haran,[11] and in Hellenistic times it was general practice to refer to Semitic gods by the names of their Greek equivalents.[12] Unfortunately, there is no evidence that foreign gods in Israel were given Hebrew names in pre-exilic times. There are, however, some indications that this did not always happen. For example, the gods brought to the old Northern Kingdom by the new settlers after 722 BC (II Kings 17.30–31) retained their foreign names in Israel. Likewise, the historian did not attempt to find a Hebrew or Canaanite equivalent for the name of the god in whose temple Sennacherib died (II Kings 19.37). The Babylonian Tammuz retained his own name in Jerusalem (Ezek. 8.14) and perhaps similarly the Mesopotamian Sakkuth and Kaiwan (Amos 5.26).[13] These few examples cannot provide a sufficient basis for the formulation of a general rule which may be applied in the present study, but at least they suggest the likelihood that any god whose worship was officially required would have been known by its Assyrian name in Israel. Hence the natural presupposition is that a god with a Canaanite name was Canaanite, unless it can be shown to have been otherwise.

Östreicher thought that the Asherah image in v. 6 was an idol of the Assyrian Ishtar,[14] but there seems to be little reason to doubt that the text refers to the Palestinian cult-symbol of the mother-goddess, or more specifically to Manasseh's Phoenician idol which was probably in some respects similar to the Asherah image erected at an earlier date by Ahab in Samaria. The terminology certainly attests to the same kind of wooden image as mentioned elsewhere in the Old Testament, one which could be carried out and burned.[15] It is recorded in v. 7 that there were women employed in the sanctuary in the weaving of garments for Asherah. However, there is nothing particularly Assyrian about this practice, for the manufacture of sacred vestments is attested, not only in Babylon,[16] but also in Syria,[17] the Greek world[18] and Ugarit.[19] Again, the $q^e d\bar{e}\check{s}\bar{i}m$ referred to in this verse are hardly functionaries of an Assyrian cult, for they are well known figures in the common Palestinian fertility cults of Old Testament times.[20] It would therefore seem fairly clear that this cult in vv. 6–7 belongs to the *milieu* of Canaanite fertility religion which was commonly associated with the names of Baal and Asherah in the Old Testament and was well established in the land from a very early date.[21] It may be that the altars which Josiah dismantled on the roof of the Upper Chamber of Ahaz and in the two courts of the Temple

(v. 12) were also dedicated to Baal and therefore belonged to the same Canaanite or Phoenician context, but they could equally well have been erected for the service of the astral gods,[22] particularly since Manasseh is said to have dedicated altars to the Host of Heaven in the two courts of the Temple (II Kings 21.5). There is, however, no evidence to suggest that the heavenly deities, if worshipped at these altars, would have been Assyrian[23] and, as will be shown later – indeed, as the evidence already collected suggests[24] – it is likely that there may have been influences other than Mesopotamian involved.

Östreicher considered that v. 11 contained strong evidence for the presence in the Temple precincts of the cult, with its own separate buildings (the *parwārīm*), of the Assyrian chief god, Ashur, whom he identified with the Sun-god Shamash.[25] But it is by no means clear that his impressions are correct and other interpretations are possible, if not preferable. Firstly as noted earlier, Shamash and Ashur were not identified with each other by the Assyrians.[26] And secondly, there is no compelling *a priori* reason for believing that the Sun-cult which Josiah abolished was Assyrian in origin. Sun-worship is well attested in every land in the ancient world from Egypt to Hatti and from Rome to Iran[27] and scholars have found many traces of solar religion in Israel itself.[28] Thus it would have been surprising if some kind of Sun-cult had not found its way into the Jerusalem Temple whether there had or had not been political pressure from Assyria.

It is customary in connection with v. 11 to make reference to the Nabonidus inscription on which Bunene is called 'the rider of the chariot' (*ra-kib* ^gis^*narkabti*) on which the Sun sits enthroned.[29] But the reference in this text is probably to the processional horses and chariots used in Mesopotamian festivals for conveying the images of the gods.[30] Most of the Assyrian gods of any importance had their processional chariots,[31] but since the solar chariot at Jerusalem is the only one mentioned it seems likely that it was more than just a piece of processional apparatus and that it is to be related to a mythology in which the Sun-god drove across the sky in a horse-drawn chariot.

Now there is plenty of evidence to suggest that the horses and chariots of the Sun in Jerusalem may be associated with both mythological beliefs and cultic usages already found amongst the Canaanites before the time of Assyrian domination. An eighth-century inscription from Zinjirli mentions a deity *rkb'l* along with Hadad, El, Reshef and Shamash.[32] The name implies that a divine charioteer[33] featured in the local[34] mythology of Zinjirli and, since his companions are mostly solar deities or gods with solar aspects,[35] it is highly probable that *rkb'l* is to be regarded as the driver of a solar chariot. In the same category is the Greek mythology of Helios who was also depicted as the rider of a horse-drawn chariot.[36] Although his functions were gradually taken over in classical Greece by Apollo, god of light, the mythology of Helios survived, particularly in the Phaethon myth[37] which seems to have been known in a modified form in Israel.[38]

Apart from the written evidence of Greece and Zinjirli, ancient literature from outside Israel appears to be devoid of an explicit Sun-chariot mythology.[39] Fortunately, however, antiquity has left other witnesses besides literature. Pottery models of horses and chariots have been found in the course of excavations at Ras Shamra and in Palestine. A model of a horse, chariot and two riders has been reconstructed from remains found at Ras Shamra. Of the horse only the head survives, but affixed to the front of the chariot is a possible solar motif and it is conceivable, if the reconstruction is correct, that the riders are the Sun-god and his charioteer.[40] Three model chariots, two with riders, were found in the tenth-century stratum at Gerar. Their style is completely different from the Ras Shamra model and can hardly be associated with anything other than the crude votive art of Palestine and the ancient Near East generally.[41] Together with these models were found a number of pottery wheels, similar to model chariot wheels, mostly pre-dating the twelfth century BC, unearthed at several Palestinian sites including Lachish, Megiddo and Beth-shan.[42] The finds themselves give little indication of their original use, but most scholars would agree that they were votive offerings.[43] Again, whilst there is no concrete proof, the likelihood is that at least some of these models belong amongst the votive offerings of a solar cult.[44] This suggestion seems more plausible in view of some recent discoveries at Jerusalem and Hazor. Model horses with solar (?) discs on their foreheads, apparently from the eighth or the seventh century BC, were found at Jerusalem,[45] and these may be compared with the terra cotta stylization of a horse's head with the solar emblem of disc and cross impressed on its forehead found in the ninth-century stratum at Hazor.[46] The style in both cases is thoroughly Palestinian and in all probability the objects are again votive offerings. Although some of these finds come from periods when direct Assyrian influence may have been possible, they are all early and witness to the presence of horses and chariots in the cult and mythology of Palestine before the seventh century BC.

In the Old Testament itself, apart from II Kings 23.11, there is no explicit statement that horses and chariot were associated with the Sun, but there is evidence that they featured in Palestinian mythology.[47] Elijah and Elisha were separated by a chariot of fire and horses of fire and, although either Yahweh or some member of the heavenly court must have been the charioteer, the association with fire immediately suggests the influence of solar imagery (II Kings 2.11–12). Elisha's words, 'the chariot of Israel and its horses',[48] whatever their particular application in the context,[49] must contain some allusion to an underlying mythology or cultic usage.[50] The *milieu* of this mythology appears to be Canaanite, for in the poem of Habakkuk, which contains elements that are indubitably very old, the psalmist describes Yahweh, in a setting which recalls the Canaanite myth of the battles against Nahr, Yam and Tehom,[51] with the words 'you ride upon your horses, your chariot is salvation'[52] (Hab. 3.8). Although the writer may have thought of the storm-cloud and the winds as the chariot and horses of Yahweh,[53] the picture is again one of light and brightness (vv. 3–4, 11), suggesting once more the possible influence of a solar mythology, as is clearly brought out in the NEB translation of vv. 3b–4:

> His radiance overspreads the skies,
> and his splendour fills the earth.
> He rises like the dawn,
> with twin rays starting forth at his side;
> the skies are the hiding-place of his majesty,
> and the everlasting ways are for his swift flight.

Furthermore, Reshef, who is here said to accompany Yahweh (v. 5). is recognizable as an attendant of the Sun elsewhere.[54] Isaiah uses similar imagery when he portrays Yahweh coming in judgment surrounded by fire and riding on a chariot (Isa. 66.15–16). There is also a later tradition that a chariot for the cherubim and the ark stood in the Temple in the days of Solomon (I Chron. 28.18) and it may be that it was this cultic object which provided the imagery for Ezekiel's vision of Yahweh's glory (Ezek. 1; 10). The 'wheels' that the prophet saw would then have been the wheels of the ark-chariot, whilst the four living creatures (1.5) or cherubim (10.15) would have played the part normally performed by horses. The context is certainly one of fire and brightness (1.4; 10.4, 7), and whilst Ezek. 10—11 describes the departure of the glory of Yahweh, it is from the east that he returns (43.2), just as a Sun-god would do. Ezekiel's mythology is inseparable from the Temple, suggesting that his language may be moulded, not by Babylonian religious practices, but by the familiar Jerusalem cultus.

Although Yahweh was hardly a solar deity, it seems that the Israelites were familiar with a mythology in which a Sun-god journeyed by horse-drawn chariot and that some of the language and imagery of this mythology has been employed in descriptions of Yahweh. This ancient conception in Israelite folk-lore, of a deity with marked solar features riding a horse and chariot, shares much more with Mediterranean than with Mesopotamian mythology. In Assyrian art the Sun-god, it seems, was symbolized as a disc transported by wings like a bird,[55] whereas the Sun-chariot motif belongs to Greece, north-west Syria and Palestine. The antiquity of the mythology suggests that only a theory of cultural intercourse at a very early date can explain its presence in the three cultures.[56] It is a short step from myth to cult, and it is therefore not at all surprising to find that the 'kings of Judah' dedicated horses and chariot to the Sun.

The horses are said to have been kept 'beside the chamber of Nathanmelech . . . which is in the *parwārīm*.' It is, however, extremely difficult to give a satisfactory explanation of the derivation and meaning of the word *parwārīm*. It has been maintained that it is the Persian word *parwār*, 'an open kiosk' or 'summer-house', in this instance referring to some open structure in the Temple area,[57] but the implication of this suggestion is that the whole phrase, *'aser bapparwārīm*, is a late gloss dating from the Persian period and is therefore of dubious historical value. It has also been proposed that *parwār* is an alternative or an erroneous spelling of the similar word, *parbār*, in I Chron. 26.18 and is to be translated 'Temple precinct' or 'forecourt', the meaning that *prbr* apparently bears in an Aramaic inscription of the fifth or fourth century BC.[58] This, however, can hardly be a correct definition, for *parbār* in I Chron. 26.18 is not a court, but a structure. Again, on the basis of the same identification with *parbār*, it has been argued that *parwārīm* must be related to the name of the Sun-temples in Sippar and Larsa, *Ebabbar* ('shining house').[59] But once more this conclusion is difficult to accept, for, apart from the problem of explaining the plural form of *parwārīm*, the *parbār* in I Chron. 26.18 stood behind the Temple at the west gate and was considered neither of pagan importation nor related to Sun-worship. Furthermore, the transformation of an original *Ebabbar* into the Hebrew *parwār* involves too many consonantal changes to be convincing.[60] Finally, it has been suggested that *parwārīm* is an Egyptian loan word, *pr wr*, meaning 'Sun-chapel' or 'Sun-barque'.[61] Although this proposal necessitates no textual emendation, relates *parwārīm* directly to the Sun-cult, and leaves the question of *parbār* in I Chron. 26.18 open, it does raise the further problem of how a word for a fairly small, portable shrine has come to designate a fixed structure of considerable size, and again it leaves the difficulty of the plural form unanswered. Amidst this variety of possible interpretations the word *parwārīm* cannot be taken to signify the presence of Assyrian solar worship, especially since the theory of Mesopotamian derivation requires emendation of the text and raises other problems.

It may now be concluded from our study of the text of Kings that there is no clear evidence that Assyrian cults were to be found amongst those that Josiah abolished from the Jerusalem Temple, let alone that they had been introduced under obligation. The material that has been adduced as evidence is either better explained in some other way, or at least is susceptible to alternative interpretation. Nevertheless, scholars have also appealed to the account of the reform of the *bāmōt* for further witness to the presence of Assyrian religion in Israel at this time and it is to this that we must now turn.

Gressmann argued that the *kemārīm* in v.5 were specially appointed priests of the Assyrian cult in Judah,[62] but there is nothing that can be found either here or elsewhere to support such a conclusion. Certainly the *kemārīm* were idolatrous or pagan priests and were distinct from the *kōhanīm* in v.8a who were Yahweh-priests permitted to come to the central sanctuary. Both here and in Zeph. 1.4 the *kemārīm* are associated with the worship of Baal and the astral deities and in Hos. 10.5 they feature as the idolatrous priests of the calf or calves of *Bēt 'āwen*.[63] It may be that the term *kōmer* is cognate with the Accadian *kumru*, 'a priest', and that it entered the Hebrew language in the period of Assyrian domination, but this supposition cannot be conclusive, nor can it be a basis for the further suggestion that the *kᵉmārīm* were Assyrian priests, for the word *kmr* occurs frequently with the meaning 'priest' in Phoenician, Punic and Aramaic inscriptions, as also in the writings and inscriptions of Elephantine, Nabataea, Palmyra and Minaea.[64] Furthermore, the common word for 'priest' in Assyria at this time was *šangû*; *kumru*, which was an Old Assyrian word for 'priest', is found in the Middle Assyrian period only once and is not attested thereafter.[65] It would therefore seem best to conclude that *kōmer* was not borrowed from the Assyrians, but that it was a widely used Semitic term to which Hebrew has given a particular slant. *Kōmer* in the Old Testament certainly denotes a priest of pagan or foreign gods, whereas in the Phoenician inscriptions the word is regularly used with no overtones of degradation.[66] Even if II Kings 23.5; Zeph. 1.4 and possibly[67] Hos. 10.5 were thought to indicate that the *kᵉmārīm* were officials of astral cults, it would still not be legitimate to draw the conclusion that association with star-gods implies Assyrian influence, since, for example, in the seventh century BC at Nerab in Syria the priest of the Moon-god, Sahr, was also known as a *kmr*.[68] As the *kᵉmārīm* in II Kings 23.5 were *bāmōt* officials, and therefore probably also priests of the fertility cults,[69] it would perhaps be more reasonable to maintain that any star-gods which they may have venerated were indigenous, for a strong affinity may be noted between the astral and fertility aspects of religion in Canaan.[70]

Besides these idolatrous priests, v. 5 includes mention of others who burned sacrifices on the *bāmōt* to Baal, the Sun, the Moon, the *mazzālōt* and all the Host of Heaven, and this has naturally been useful material for those seeking traces of Assyrian religion in Judah in Josiah's reign. But reference must again be made to the Zakir inscription from Afis which lists the gods Baalshamem, Shamash, Sahr, the gods of heaven and the gods of earth in that order and which may be used as evidence that the deities in II Kings 23.5 are in all probability Canaanite or Syro-Phoenician.[71] Baal is well known in the fertility cults of the *bāmōt* in pre-exilic Israel.[72] *Šemeš* and *Yārēaḥ* were Semitic gods, but the use of these terms here gives little indication of the provenance of the gods, for they are also common Hebrew for Sun and Moon respectively. *Šemeš* and its cognates were widely used in the Semitic world to designate both Sun and Sun-god(dess). The Ugaritic *špš* and the Arabian *šams* were goddesses and in Syria and Mesopotamia *šamaš* was a god, but *šemeš* in the Old Testament could be masculine or feminine[73] and there is nothing to suggest the gender of the deity in v. 5. *Yārēaḥ* is more properly the Moon or Moon-god of Syria-Palestine[74] and it is noteworthy that whilst *Šamaš* was the name of the Sun-god in Assyria, the Accadian *arḫu*, 'the Moon', is not used even as an epithet of the Moon-god.[75] There is thus no self-evident reason why these gods should be regarded as Assyrian and since, as gods worshipped on the *bāmōt*, they are probably to be associated with the local fertility cults,[76] they may best be compared with *špš* and *yrḫ*, both of whom are active in the fertility myths of ancient Ugarit.[77] The Babylonian Shamash, in contrast, was not primarily a fertility god, but the god of justice, right and truth.[78] And yet the invective against the devotees of the Sun and the astral cults in Jer. 8.1–3 is part of a sermon which castigates the men of Judah for their singular lack of interest in such matters as justice and truth.

Identification of the *mazzālōt* in II Kings 23.5 is subject to continuing debate and obscurity, for the Semitic cognates differ considerably in meaning[79] and the Versions vary widely in interpretation.[80] The variety of suggested identifications in recent writings both attests and adds to this confusion.[81] Several scholars have favoured the proposal that the *mazzālōt* is the Zodiac and that the cult in v. 5 is therefore of Assyrian origin, but it now seems that the Zodiac as it is known today, with twelve signs, was first determined in the fifth century BC.[82] Furthermore, the Accadian *mazzaltu* does not mean 'Zodiac', nor is it used of the belt of stars that forms the Zodiac.[83] There is no evidence that the Assyrians worshipped the Zodiac[84] and it is therefore unlikely that the *mazzālōt* revered by Josiah's subjects had anything to do with this particular circle of stars, or at least not as it was later known in Babylonia and elsewhere. Alternatively, some commentators have wished to identify the *mazzālōt* with one or all of the planets. This is a much more acceptable suggestion, for the planets were worshipped all over the ancient Near East, but if it is correct, the implication is that the influence could not have been Assyrian. The Accadian word for 'planet' is *bibbu*, or even *kakkabu*, but not *mazzaltu.*[85] A third and perhaps equally fruitful line of investigation proposes the identification of *mazzālōt* with *mazzārōt* in Job 38.32.[86] In the latter passage *mazzārōt* is not a planet, but one particular constellation with seasonal rising and setting, as is signified by the accompanying word, *beʿittō* (in its season).[87] It may therefore be argued that *mazzārōt* was the name of some important seasonal constellation in Israel which, in II Kings 23.5, has been applied by extension to the major constellations in general, just as *kesīl* (Orion) has been used of all the constellations in the phrase 'the stars of heaven and their constellations (lit. their Orions, *kesīlēhem*)' in Isa. 13.10. On these grounds it may be maintained that *mazzālōt*, as it is used in II Kings 23.5, is virtually synonymous with 'Host of Heaven'.[88] But if this suggestion is correct, it is difficult to see how the use of the term *mazzālōt* in this passage can be understood to reflect Assyrian influence.

A further *bāmā*, located at one of the city gates, is mentioned in v. 8b, but it is extremely difficult to define the nature of its cult. Recently J. Gray has argued that its worship was directed towards the propitiation of the guardian deities of the city gate, 'perhaps . . . bull-colossi which represent the guardian genii of the entrance in Assyrian palaces'. This suggestion is difficult to assess, since it is based on unsupported textual emendation.[89] Others have preferred the alternative emendation which gives the translation '*bāmā* of the Satyrs'[90] and this proposal can claim the additional support of II Chron. 11.15, which records the institution of a cult of the Satyrs by Jeroboam, and Lev. 17.7 (H), which prohibits their worship. By contrast, whilst Assyrian bull-colossi were considered to be numinous, there appears to be no evidence of any kind of cult or act of worship associated with them. Thus, though it may well be that bull-colossi did stand by one or more of the Jerusalem gates, it is not likely that the cult of the gate-*bāmā* which Josiah destroyed was associated with these figures through Assyrian influence.

The Molech cult (v. 10) is shrouded in obscurity and even the location of the cult place, the *tōpet* in the Valley of *Ben-Hinnōm*, is subject to debate.[91] But the primary cause of uncertainty in describing the origins and background of the cult is the difficulty in identifying the god. Partly because the Hebrew *gēʾ hinnōm* (Hinnom Valley) was later used as a name for hell (Gehenna), it has usually been thought that Molech, whose name is spelt with the vowels of *bōšet* (shame), was an underworld god, but in recent decades it has been disputed whether Molech was a god-name at all. Eissfeldt argues that there was originally no god called Molech, since *mlk* appears as a common noun meaning 'sacrifice' in the phrases *mlk'mr* (sacrifice of a lamb) and *mlk'dm* (sacrifice of a man) in late Punic and Phoenician inscriptions.[92] On the other hand, the words *dbḥ.mlk* (sacrifice of *mlk*?) found in an Ugaritic text in conjunction with *dbḥ.ṣpn* (sacrifice of Saphon) and *dbḥ.bʿl* (sacrifice of Baal) may suggest, although the interpretation of the text is debated, that *mlk* was a divine name in early Canaan.[93] A possible connection with a Mesopotamian underworld god, Malik, has been suggested,[94] but Cazelles, whilst admitting this possibility, believes that the evidence points to Phoenician rather than Mesopotamian influence. He suggests that the term *mlk* was first introduced to Israel through Phoenicia with the general meaning of 'offering', but was misinterpreted at an early date, perhaps by confusion with the name of the Ammonite god, Milkom.[95] Despite this uncertainty and diversity of opinion, there are several good reasons for believing that the Molech cult, even though the earliest reference to it in the Old Testament is in the Assyrian period, was not of Assyrian importation, but that it probably belonged, like most of the other cults we have already studied, to the common paganism of the eastern Mediterranean seaboard. Firstly, whatever its original significance, by the time of Josiah the rite of the Hinnom Valley was one of sacrifice by burning. The formula most widely used in the Old Testament to describe this rite, as here in II Kings 23.10, is *lᵉhaʿᵃbîr 'et-bᵉnō wᵉ'et-bittō bā'ēš lammōlek*,[96] 'to pass his son and his daughter over (through, in?) the fire to Molech (or, as an offering)'. Once the more general verb *nātan* (give) is used in place of *ʿābar* (Lev. 20.2–5). It has therefore been argued that the rite was non-sacrificial, since *lᵉhaʿᵃbîr* signifies a ritual of initiation by passing the child over the flames.[97] However, there are a number of passages where the verb *śārap* (burn) is used and these must leave no doubt that the rite was one of sacrifice by burning,[98] and, as has already been noted, sacrifice by burning was not an Assyrian practice.[99] Furthermore, it was child sacrifice[100] and this also was not an Assyrian practice, but much rather one found amongst the Phoenicians.[101] Indeed it may even have been similar to the child sacrifice of Carthage which is so well attested by archaeological remains and in ancient literature.[102] Moreover, whilst there was an underworld god Malik in ancient Mesopotamia, there is no evidence that child sacrifices or fire offerings were ever made to him, but the Phoenician and Punic sources do, as has been seen, suggest such rites in connection with the sacrificial term *mlk*. Finally, whether there ever was a god Molech in Judah or not, at least the Old Testament strongly suggests that the deity honoured in the Hinnom rites was Canaanite.[103] Jeremiah (2.23; 19.5; 32.35) even witnesses to a belief that this deity was Baal, for whom an altar had been erected in the Hinnom Valley, and also to the popular belief that the cult conformed to the will of Yahweh (7.31).[104] In view of these various considerations it seems highly unlikely that the background to this cult is Assyrian, much less that it was an official imposition, but in the present state of our knowledge it is difficult to formulate more positive conclusions about its place of origin. A number of scholars have suggested possible associations with different stars and planets, but again opinion is so divided and the evidence is so limited that no certain conclusions can be reached, although some of these suggestions remain possibilities which merit further evaluation.[105]

Finally, II Kings 23.13 relates the desecration of *bāmōt* dedicated to Ashtoreth, Kemosh and Milkom situated east of Jerusalem. I Kings 11.5–7 describes the founding of these cults and attributes their introduction to Solomon's foreign marriages. There can therefore be no question of Assyrian influence here, all the more so since the deities are specifically defined as the national gods of Sidon, Moab and Ammon respectively. As the cult places are said to have been located to the east of Jerusalem, they must have stood on one of the summits of the Mount of Olives. But the further information is given that they were to the south of the Hill of the Destroyer (*har hammašḥīt*). Most commentators argue that the name of this hill is a pun on, or a textual corruption of *har hammišḥā*, the Mount of Anointing (that is, the Mount of Olives), but the term *hammašḥīt* may equally well be of mythological significance. The same word is used of the destroying angel in the account of the tenth Egyptian plague (Ex. 12) and in the report of the scourge that swept the land following David's census (II Sam. 24.16; I Chron. 21.15). Furthermore, the Mount of Olives also had mythological associations in ancient Israel, perhaps originally of a non-Yahwistic nature. Here David worshipped some unspecified god (II Sam. 15.30ff.), thither went the Glory of Yahweh on leaving the Temple (Ezek. 11.23) and thence it returned (Ezek. 43.1ff.), and it was this hill that featured as the place of exit from the underworld in the apocalypse of Zechariah (14.1-4). According to the Old Testament records this mythological complex pre-dates the advent of the Assyrians by several centuries and it is therefore most unlikely that the term *hammašḥīt* in any way cloaks an allusion to an Assyrian god. It has, however, been maintained that the gods that Josiah expelled from this site were associated with one or other of the planets, and if the arguments have any substance,[106] Ashtoreth, Kemosh and Milkom may be regarded as non-Assyrian members of the Host of Heaven.

In view of the foregoing study it must be concluded that there is no clear evidence that Josiah carried out a purge of Assyrian gods on the hill-shrines and other local sanctuaries of Judah. On the other hand, there is good reason to believe that some such purge would have been an integral part of the campaign at Bethel and other Northern cities (II Kings 23.15-20). There must have been some kind of anti-Assyrian motivation for this campaign, even if many other factors were involved, for Samaria was at this time still an Assyrian province in fact, if not in power, and any sortie into its territory must have been regarded as an open act of military rebellion. However, the extent of Josiah's intervention in Samaria is extremely difficult to determine[107] and there is nothing to indicate that an anti-Assyrian iconoclasm was one of his main objectives. Whilst it is known that Assyrian and other foreign cults were patronized by the new settlers in Samaria (II Kings 17.30-1), there is not even a hint that these were the primary objects of Josiah's purge. Whatever may have motivated the Northern campaign, the account of it in vv. 15-20 is written in stereotyped Deuteronomic language which prohibits detailed investigation and leaves no impression whatsoever of a purge of Assyrian gods. Likewise, II Kings 23.24, the postscript to Josiah's reforms, makes no allusion to anything that could be regarded as particularly Assyrian. The terminology is thoroughly Israelite and the proscribed divinatory and pagan media are all known to have been found in the land at a much earlier date, well before the advent of the Assyrians.[108] Thus it must be concluded that, if Assyrian gods were worshipped on the *bāmōt*, whether of Judah or of Israel, they did not impress themselves on the historiographer as being noteworthy marks of apostasy, and hence it is unlikely that their cults were officially imposed by the Assyrians as symbols of vassal status.

Several scholars have attempted to find at least a modicum of unity in the paganism which was abolished in Josiah's reign by determining a number of official Assyrian cults, but virtually all the cultic apparatus removed from the Temple and the land may be associated with well-established Palestinian, Canaanite, Syrian and Phoenician religion both of contemporary and also of earlier periods. The details of Josiah's reforms, whilst full of allusions that are difficult to define precisely, may be more correctly interpreted in terms of a general purge of a wide diversity of cults. The very fact that the Assyrian gods were not considered worthy of special mention in the account of the reforms suggests that they neither enjoyed a privileged status in the Judaean cult, nor formed a peculiar focus for the reformation. No clear indication was found that Ahaz or Manasseh were compelled to introduce Mesopotamian cults to Judah and, even if anti-Assyrian sentiment aided Josiah in some aspects of his purges (a fact which, considering the historical situation, can hardly be doubted), it seems that Östreicher's thesis must now be considerably modified. Political factors were, of course, very important, for they set the tenor of the age. Assyria was on the decline and her empire slowly crumbling. As in the days of Hezekiah, the hope for independence began to rise again, and no doubt the rebirth of nationalistic expectation did much to promote the demand for a strong, purified and united national cult. Men were once more prepared to listen to those who called upon them to stand by the cause of Yahweh. Both Zephaniah and Jeremiah spared no words in condemning the paganism of their day and in warning of the consequences of continued apostasy.[109] In an earlier age their teaching might have been stifled or gone unheeded, but now there were those who were ready to hear and obey. The time was ripe for both rebellion and reform. Nevertheless, the call to reform was not primarily political, but religious, for it was voiced above all by those men who stood behind the law-book which was produced in 622 BC. The importance of the movement which these men represent for the study of the causes of Josiah's reforms is clearly signified by the fact that it produced the book used by Josiah himself and later edited the most authoritative account of the reformation that we possess. If these arguments are correct, that the reformation, however much aided by the revolt against Assyria, was not *per se* an act of rebellion, then it is perhaps now necessary to think again about the degree of influence and authority that was carried by *Urdeuterononium*, and more particularly by the people behind it, and to reassess its place among the causes of the reformation. But here we begin to go beyond the scope of the present study.[110]

VI

ASTRAL BELIEFS IN JUDAH AND
THE ANCIENT WORLD

Whilst a growing number of scholars, as has been seen, are putting forward criticisms of Östreicher and his more extravagant followers, there are as yet only a few who would deny completely the presence of officially imposed Assyrian cults in Judah. As the various recorded aspects of Judaean paganism come to be recognized as non-Assyrian, there is an increasing tendency to resort to a statement that the astral gods, particularly the Host of Heaven, represent the Assyrian official presence. It is argued that this must be the case, since the many references to the worship of the Host of Heaven, the record of the worship of the Queen of Heaven and the possible allusion to astrology in the Old Testament are all limited to the period of Assyrian domination; and it is well known that there was plenty of astral learning in Assyria. This argument often represents a retreat to a gap in our knowledge, for the Host of Heaven is never defined or illustrated by examples and could therefore be any group of star-gods, Assyrian or otherwise. The argument from limitation to the Assyrian period is open to the same kind of criticism, for it could also be applied to other material from any book of the Assyrian era or its aftermath.[1] In view of the weakness of these generalized arguments, it seems fitting to re-examine the assertions that the astral gods were Assyrian and that their worship was officially imposed.

From Jer. 7.17–18; 44.16–19 we learn that the Queen of Heaven[2] was worshipped in Judah at the end of the seventh century. This goddess has been identified with the Moon[3] and the Sun,[4] but is most commonly thought to have been the Babylonian Ishtar, one of whose titles, *šarrat šamê*, means precisely 'Queen of Heaven'.[5]

However, there were other goddesses in the ancient world who held this title. For example, the Hurrian Ḫebat, who was identified with the Hittite Sun-goddess of Arinna, was known as Queen of Heaven,[6] and on an Egyptian stele from Bethshan Anat is called 'Lady of Heaven, Mistress of All the Gods'.[7] Therefore the name Queen of Heaven itself cannot be allowed to prejudice the discussion in favour of identification with the Assyrian goddess and it can hardly be taken to indicate that her cult was part of an obligation laid on Judah by her overlord.

There are a number of archaeological finds which show that the Palestinian mother-goddess in her own right had astral attributes before the time of Assyrian domination. They are all of the same artistic quality and the crudeness of some of them may suggest a popular, rather than a priestly origin. A roughly hewn, assymetrical, six-pointed star was found on the wall of one of the rooms of the temple of Anat at Megiddo,[8] and this, together with the Bethshan stele, would seem to indicate that Anat, who is now well known from the Ugaritic texts as a fertility goddess active in the restoration of Baal, was sometimes regarded as an astral deity. Confirmation for this conclusion would appear to come from a plaque found at *Tell eṣ-Ṣāfi* in the Shephelah on which is depicted the figure of a typically Palestinian mother-goddess (possibly Anat, but this cannot be certain) with an Egyptian Hathor hair-style, holding a serpent in each hand. Two stars, a hexagram and a pentagram, are impressed in the field or background.[9] The same motif of a star in the field is to be seen on a votive altar from Gezer, which is roughly contemporary with the *Tell eṣ-Ṣāfi* plaque, belonging to the period of the monarchy.[10] In the foreground is a lion being slain, and on its shoulder is imprinted a second star.[11] Perhaps this second star should be identified with the 'King Star' (*mul*LUGAL), Regulus, which stands on the shoulder of the astral lion, the constellation Leo.[12] The antiquity and importance of the astral lion in mythology and art is now well attested,[13] and although Regulus itself is not a particularly outstanding star, being the faintest of the first magnitude, it commands a position of some eminence standing, as it does, on the shoulder of the Lion. It was also closely related by its position on the zodiacal belt with the summer solstice,[14] and was therefore associated with one of the major stages in the annual cycle, and hence with fertility. Thus it would have been natural to associate Leo with the mother-goddess, and this may well be the explanation of the scene depicted on the Gezer altar. The star in the field is probably, after the pattern of the *Tell eṣ-Ṣāfi* plaque, the symbol of the mother-goddess who is seen to accompany the Lion of summer, her astral companion. This conclusion is supported by a bronze plaque from Ras Shamra on which the mother-goddess is portrayed standing on the back of a lion which has a star imprinted on its shoulder.[15] The mother-goddess, as well as caring for the crops of the soil, cares also for the beasts of the field; she is the πότνια θηρῶν,[16] as symbolized by her association with the Lion, the constellation of midsummer.[17]

It may now be safely concluded that the mother-goddess was associated with some star or planet very early in the history of fertility religion in Palestine. She was represented as an astral deity at Ugarit, Megiddo, Gezer, Bethshan and *Tell eṣ-Ṣāfi* before the time of Assyrian domination and it is in no way surprising to discover that, perhaps because of an association with the King Star, Regulus, she was known in Palestine as the Queen of Heaven. It is therefore preferable that she should be seen in a wider context than officially imposed Assyrian cults in seventh-century Judah.[18] Indeed, it can hardly be maintained that her cult belonged to any scheme of official religion, for it was located, not in the Temple or any other kind of state sanctuary, but in 'the cities of Judah and in the streets of Jerusalem' (Jer. 7.17; 44.17). Her worship was local and popular, without priesthood or sanctuary, and must be ranked with common superstitition and the thousands of mother-goddess plaques from archaeological sites throughout Palestine.[19]

If the conclusion is correct that the cult of the Queen of Heaven was part of the vulgar religion of the day, it must be equally correct to see the cult of the Host of Heaven in the same setting. If it were true that the worship of the Host of Heaven 'came in with the Assyrian domination as part of the obligation of subject states to the empire',[20] there would surely have been some trace left in the Old Testament of the adoption of the kind of astral beliefs that were particularly prominent in Mesopotamia, but there is nothing to indicate that it is possible to differentiate between the beliefs about the heavenly bodies held in Israel and in ancient Near Eastern paganism generally.

Whilst it seems that the serious study of mathematical astronomy in Mesopotamia was a development of the Persian era,[21] the

Assyrians, Babylonians and Sumerians had for long been interested in the celestial bodies. They had begun to assemble some observational information[22] and had accumulated an extensive collection of astrological lore.[23] They also personified some of the more outstanding heavenly bodies as gods; the Moon was personified as Sin, the Sun as Shamash and Venus as Ishtar. With the passage of time the anthropomorphic aspects of these gods increased in importance and the corresponding heavenly bodies came to be recognized as their symbols.[24] But whilst other aspects of these gods came very much to the fore – for example, Shamash was also god of justice and Ishtar goddess of fertility and war[25] – Sin, Shamash and Ishtar continued to be the deities of the Moon, the Sun and Venus respectively. Some of the other gods had secondary astral associations; for example, Nergal, god of the underworld, pestilence and war, was associated with Mars, and Ninurta, god of war and fertility, with Saturn.[26] The stars and constellations were often regarded as numinous and powerful in magic and astrology and could be invoked in prayer.[27] Observation of the stars and planets therefore played a not inconsiderable role in Mesopotamian religious circles. Whilst there are inevitably some similarities between these Mesopotamian beliefs and what is known of Judaean star-worship, the differences are also considerable. In particular there is little evidence that the people of Judah showed any interest in the kind of astrological observation that stood as the very centre of Mesopotamian astral beliefs. As far as it is possible to determine from the sources available, Judean astronomy was largely limited to seasonal observation, probably for calendrical and agricultural purposes,[28] and there is only one verse in the Old Testament (Jer. 10.2) which could suggest the influence of Mesopotamian astrology during the seventh century BC, but even there the allusion is by no means clear.[29]

On the other hand, there can be no question that the Sun, the Moon and perhaps Venus were worshipped in Judah, but the mere existence of such cults cannot by itself be regarded as evidence of Assyrian influence, for these phenomena had their equivalent gods amongst almost every one of Israel's neighbours. None the less, it can hardly be doubted that in this age of vassaldom Assyrian influence must have contributed much to the upsurge of the astral cults in Palestine. It may have been because of Assyrian influence that Manasseh erected altars in the Temple courts to the Host of Heaven (II Kings 21.5) and that cultic vessels were dedicated to their worship in the Temple itself (II Kings 23.4). And yet there is little reason to believe that these deities honoured in the Temple were in any way different from the Host of Heaven whose cult is otherwise said to be mainly local and popular. The devotees are known to have worshipped on the roofs of houses (Jer. 19.13; Zeph. 1.5), on the local *bāmōt* (II Kings 23.5) and in the villages of Judah (Deut. 17.2–3).[30] Thus, whilst there is evidence that the star-cults were given royal support, the general impression remains that these (including the cults in the Temple and precincts) were little more than popular, local manifestations of the kind of superstitious astral religion which was found almost everywhere in ancient Near Eastern paganism. The influence of such astral beliefs from amongst Israel's more immediate neighbours has already been noted several times[31] and can hardly be questioned, particularly if the Deuteronomist's statement can be trusted that *all* Israel's neighbours (*kōl hā'ammîm taḥat kol-haššāmāyim*) were in some respect star-worshippers and that the influence of each and every one of them, not just of the Assyrians or the Babylonians, was to be feared in Judah (Deut. 4.19).

Astral gods were widely venerated in Southern Arabia and, although the evidence is not so extensive, it seems that similar cults were also to be found in Northern and Central Arabia.[32] In the southern region in particular the supreme triad was the Moon-god, the Sun-goddess and Venus, who bore different names in different localities.[33] Amongst other stars and planets held in honour were Sirius, Canopus, Leo, the Pleiades, the Hyades, Mercury, Saturn and Jupiter.[34] Each of these astral bodies was believed to have an earthly counterpart, a *jinn* or demon, who inhabited plants, trees, rocks, etc. Athtar (Venus), the supreme god of all South Arabia, was a god of irrigation and fertility,[35] and a late, though questionable, tradition suggests that child sacrifice may have been offered to him.[36]

At the head of the official state pantheon of the Hittites stood the 'Sun-goddess of Arinna, Queen of the Land of Hatti, Queen of Heaven and Earth'.[37] Her husband, the 'Storm-god of Hatti', took second place, but in the local cults he was often chief deity.[38] There were also several further Sun-gods and -goddesses,[39] and a Moon-god, Arma, with whom various other lunar deities were identified, was worshipped particularly in the south-eastern region of Asia Minor.[40] It is not known whether Ishtar, who appears both as a god and a goddess, retained an astral aspect amongst the Hittites, but this seems not improbable, considering the Mesopotamian background from which 'she' originally came.[41]

In Egypt the Sun reigned supreme. The head of the Heliopolitan pantheon was Atum, creator of the gods and men,[42] identified with the Sun-god, Re, one of the oldest of the gods of Egypt.[43] The most extensively worshipped was the god Amun, head of the Theban pantheon, also identified with Re.[44] The chief lunar deity was Thoth, god of learning, measuring and time, with whom were identified the lunar gods, Khensu and Aah.[45] Moon-worship, however, never attained much importance and faded before the might of the Sun, just as did the cults which associated the stars and the major constellations with gods.[46]

The mythological texts from Ras Shamra have shown that the Ugaritic pantheon included a series of astral deities. The Sun-goddess, *špš*, daughter of El, 'light of the gods' and messenger of the gods, assists Anat in the restoration of Baal, thus playing her part in the cycle of fertility.[47] Likewise, the poem celebrating the marriage of *yrḫ* and *nkl*, two lunar deities, reveals that the Moon-god and Moon-goddess were deeply involved in the fertility religion of the age.[48] Again, the poem about 'the gracious gods' places *šḥr* and *šlm*, Venus as the morning and evening star, firmly in the fertility cultus.[49] It is still open to question whether *ʿttr* in the Ras Shamra texts is an astral deity like his namesake in Arabia,[50] but some scholars would compare him with *Hēlēl ben-Šaḥar* in Isa. 14.12–15, who is Venus as the morning star.[51] As in Mesopotamia, so in Ugarit there were astronomers and astrologers; *pġt* was said to 'know the courses of the stars',[52] and an astrological text has been found.[53] The phrase *ṣbủ.špš* (var. *ṣbả, ṣbê, ṣbêả*) appears five times in the Ugaritic literature[54] and has been thought to suggest the background to the Hebrew 'Host of Heaven'.[55] But, although this phrase has been translated 'host of the Sun', a number of scholars now prefer the translation 'sunset'.[56] Nevertheless, the fixed stars (*kbkbm.knm*) are grouped together with the Sun as objects of sacrificial worship in the poem in honour of *šḥr* and *šlm*[57] and it therefore remains a possibility, particularly since the Sun, the Moon and the stars in Mesopotamia are never called an army or host,[58] that the Ras Shamra texts do provide some kind

of clue to the background of the Old Testament 'Host of Heaven'.
This also seems more probable in view of the constant association
of the astral bodies with fertility in Ugarit and the Old Testament,
and also in view of the fact that the term 'Host of Heaven' was
already in use in Israel before the advent of the Assyrians.[59]

Turning to Judah's more immediate neighbours, two Philistine
gods only are known from the Old Testament, Dagon of Ashdod
and Beelzebub of Ekron, and neither of these is known to have
had astral associations.[60] But Herodotus says that a temple at
Ashkelon dedicated to ἡ Οὐρανία Ἀφροδίτη was the oldest of all the
temples of Aphrodite,[61] and his information has been supported by
the discovery of an inscription from Delos, dedicated by a certain
Damon of Ashkelon to Zeus, Ἀστάρτη Παλαιστίνη and Ἀφροδίτη
Οὐρανία[62] In Graeco-Roman mythology and religion Aphrodite,
who was equated with Astarte in Syria and Palestine, was identified with Venus, the brightest of the planets.[63]

It is difficult to describe Kemosh more fully than as the war-god
of Moab,[64] but there are some indications that the celestial bodies
were worshipped in Moab. The occurrence of the name ʿštr[65] on
the Moabite Stone and the symbols of the Sun and the Moon on
the *Baluʿa* stele point to some kind of astral beliefs.[66] Van Zyl
compares the figurine of a god on horseback with ʿAzizū,[67] who
in Palmyrene religion was identified with Venus as the morning
star[68] and with Castor in Gemini.[69]

The chief gods of the Tyrian pantheon in the seventh century
BC were Asherat-Bethel and Baalshamem, Anat and Baal-ṣaphon,
Melqart and Ashtart.[70] Of these Ashtart may have been the
Tyrian counterpart of Ishtar-Venus, since, according to Philo of
Byblos, 'the Phoenicians say that Astarte is Aphrodite'.[71] The
Phoenician Asherah may also have had astral features, since she
was later called *Asteria*, 'the Bestarred'.[72] It has been suggested also
that some form of solar worship was found in Tyre in association
with the god Melqart.[73]

In ancient Syria the gods Reshef, *Rkbʾl*, Shamash and perhaps a
solar El have already been encountered at Zinjirli,[74] and Baalshamem, Shamash, Sahr and the gods of heaven at Afis.[75] In
Hellenistic times the supreme triad at Baʿalbek was Jupiter, Venus
and Mercury, corresponding to Hadad, Atargatis and Simios,
which may, though not necessarily, be indicative of astral aspects
in these Syrian gods in an earlier age.[76] In the same way, the god of

Emesa was later identified with the Sun and his cult was super-
vised by a *sacerdos dei solis Elagabali*.[77]

In view of this widespread diffusion of belief in the divinity of
the heavenly bodies amongst Israel's neighbours in the ancient
Near East, it should not be merely assumed that the cult of the
Host of Heaven in the Old Testament is an Assyrian importation.
Indeed, the impression is that Israel's astral cults, which would
appear to have been based in superstitious veneration of the
celestial bodies rather than in observation of their movements for
the determination of astrological *omina*, stood much closer to the
cults of her immediate neighbours than to the astral aspects of
Mesopotamian religion. If this is a correct impression, there ought
to be traces of indigenous solar, lunar and astral religious beliefs
in Israel prior to the time of Assyrian conquest. And this evidence
is most certainly to be found.

Worship of the Sun is mentioned in Ezek. 8.16; 11.1 (?); Job
31.26-7, as well as in several passages already discussed in the foregoing chapters, and scholars have found many further traces of it
throughout the Old Testament. Analysis of personal and place
names, study of religious terminology, consideration of the
orientation of the Temple, examination of Temple rituals, festivals and cultic apparatus, and the relating of archaeological finds
to the information given in the Old Testament have all contributed
to a total picture which supports the belief that Sun-worship was
deeply rooted in early Israel. The subject has been so well ex-
plored that there is little to be added here.[78] Nevertheless, it has
also been thought that the *lmlk* jar-handle stamps may furnish
evidence that the Assyrians demanded recognition of the authority
of their Sun-god, or at least his symbol, from the people of Judah.
Aharoni has argued that the four-winged scarab impression show-
ing Egyptian influence dates from Hezekiah's reign before the
Assyrian invasion of 701 BC, but that after that date either Hezekiah
or Manasseh was obliged to adopt the two-winged flying disc,
'the royal insignia of Assyria'.[79] However, it would seem that the
change of insignia, in his opinion, was less of religious than of
political significance. Be that as it may, Aharoni's view of the date
of the two-winged stamps is not generally accepted. The con-
sensus of current opinion is that these stamps come from the
reign of Josiah, and therefore from the period of Assyrian decline.[80]
It has also been pointed out that, since vassal kings in the empire

were not usually stripped of their trappings of royalty, it is unlikely that an Assyrian monarch would have attempted to control
the use of a vassal's royal seal in this way.[81] Furthermore, it has
been shown that the style of the two-winged Sun-disc on the
Judaean jar handles is Syro-Phoenician rather than Assyrian.[82] It
would therefore seem that the *lmlk* seals should not be regarded as
evidence for the imposition of Assyrian solar beliefs or religious
practice in Judah and, since the two-winged Sun-disc symbol was
widely used in the ancient Near East, they are probably to be
regarded only as further evidence of an indigenous Palestinian
solar mythology.[83]

Studies in Israelite Moon-worship are hampered from the start
by the paucity and obscurity of the Old Testament information.
Outside the literature of the Assyrian period, an explicit statement
that the Moon was worshipped occurs only in Job 31.26–7, but
there are signs that the Israelites, like other ancient peoples, had
regarded the Moon with veneration from earliest times. Moon-
pendants (*śah^{a}rōnim*) are mentioned in Judg. 8.21, 26; Isa. 3.18
and are now illustrated by archaeological finds from various
sites.[84] Jericho may have been a city of the cult of the Moon[85]
and the personal names Jarah, Jaroah and Hodesh may point to
some kind of worship of or superstitious attitude to the Moon.[86]
Isaiah describes the overthrow of the Moon (*lebānā*) in an escha-
tological battle between Yahweh and the Host of Heaven (24.23),
the Psalmist feared the suffering that the Moon could inflict
(121.6), and the wisdom writers suggest that the period of the
waning Moon was unpropitious for the conduct of business
(Prov. 7.20).[87] The day of the New Moon (*ḥōdeš*) was an occasion
of religious observance in ancient Israel. At the New Moon the
king's courtiers were required to dine with him (I Sam. 20.18ff.)
and the trumpet was blown in the Temple, because it was a time
of festival (Ps. 81.4, EVV 3). New Moon and Sabbath appear together as appropriate times for consulting a prophet (II Kings 4.23)
and as occasions of restricted trade (Amos 8.5) or of special sacrifices (Isa. 1.13). The New Moon is also coupled with the appointed
feasts (*mō'adīm*), or with both the Sabbath and the appointed feasts,
as times of mirth (Hos. 2.13, EVV 11) and of special religious
observance (I Chron. 23.31; II Chron. 2.3, EVV 4; 8.13; 31.3;
Ezra 3.5; Neh. 10.34, EVV 33; Ezek. 45.17; 46.1–6). Because they
were abused, the New Moon festivals were condemned by the

early prophets (Amos. 8.5; Hos. 2.11; Isa. 1.13). It is most probable that the origins of the New Moon festival lie in the obscure past of lunar religion,[88] possibly in the wilderness period,[89] and although the festival was incorporated into Yahwism, the old taboos, rituals and fears persisted until a late time when the *ḥōdeš* became solely of calendrical significance.

Throughout the foregoing chapters deliberate emphasis has been laid on indications of both foreign and indigenous star-cults in Judah. It has been argued that Ahaz's roof altars may have been erected for the worship of Palestinian (astral ?) deities, that Manasseh's *semel* may have been dedicated to the Phoenician Astarte (but more probably to Asherah) who is associated with Venus, that a plot of land in Jerusalem was dedicated to the Arabian *Al-ʿUzzā* who is Venus as the morning star, that the Host of Heaven associated with Baal and Asherah in the Jerusalem Temple and on the Judaean *bāmōt* may have been Syro-Phoenician or indigenous, that the *kemārīm* in Josiah's time may have been priests of Canaanite star-cults, the *mazzālōt* was probably a Canaanite or Israelite term for the planets or the Host of Heaven revered by Josiah's subjects, that the god of the Hinnom cult may have been a Phoenician god associated with the planet Saturn, that Ashtoreth of the Sidonians, worshipped on the Mount of Olives from Solomonic times, was probably associated with the planet Venus, and that the Queen of Heaven was the Canaanite Anat.[90] Even though some of these identifications are based on fairly slender evidence, there now seems little reason to doubt that the Israelites did have an astral lore and mythology which was not entirely borrowed from Mesopotamia. Indeed, there are a number of archaeological finds which suggest that Palestine had its own independent astral beliefs from very early times. A wall fresco of astral significance at the late Stone Age settlement of *Telēlāt Ghassūl*, north-west of the Dead Sea, gives what is perhaps the earliest indication of interest in the stars in Palestine.[91] From Gezer of the Amarna age comes a tablet bearing signs resembling those on Mesopotamian boundary stones, some of which have been held to be star symbols. However, this tablet may be Mesopotamian in origin and hence not permissible as evidence in the present discussion.[92] Several examples of star-pendants, perhaps ear-rings, have been found at various sites in Palestine and these, like the Sun-pendants and Moon-pendants already mentioned, were probably prophylactic trinkets worn by devotees of the heavenly bodies.[93] From the period of the Judaean monarchy come the *Tell es-Ṣafi* plaque, the Anat star at Megiddo, the Gezer altar[94] and a potsherd from *El-Jib* inscribed with a hexagram framing a stylized bird.[95] The motif on this last find is probably a symbol of the mother-goddess, since several birds, particularly the swallow and the dove, were sacred to her in the ancient world.[96] A much older fragment of decorated pottery from Gaza shows a bird with a star on its wing and this may be an alternative version of the same motif.[97] Further examples of stars drawn or scratched on seals and pottery could be cited,[98] but it is often a matter of conjecture whether these had any religious significance. These few discoveries may not witness to a rich abundance of astral cults in Palestine, but neither does the Old Testament. None the less, they remove all possible doubt about the existence of star-worship in Palestine before the Assyrian period. On the whole it would appear that, even though some of these objects were found in or near various shrines, their generally rather crude art forms are further evidence for the conclusion already reached on other grounds, that veneration of the stars in early Israel was by and large a form of popular religion, often little better than superstition.

The names given by the Hebrews to the more outstanding stars and constellations are for the most part *sui generis* and often bear little or no resemblance to the Mesopotamian star names, that is, as far as it is possible to identify them.[99] Thus Aldebaran and the Hyades were known in Israel as 'the Moth' ('*āš/ʿayîš*; Job 9.9; 38.32), but in Babylonia as 'the Cheek of the Bull' (*mulis lê*) or 'the Tiara of Anu' (*mulagî ᵈanim*). The Israelites named Ursa Major 'the Winnowing-fan' (*mᵉzārîm*; Job 37.9), but ₁the Babylonians called it 'the Cart' (*mulmar-gíd-da*). It is thought that Canis Major and its bright star, Sirius, were regarded by the Israelites as animals of some kind, perhaps dogs, and were known as 'the Evil Ones' (*rᵉšāʿîm*) or 'the Hairy Ones' (*śᵉʿîrîm*; Job. 38.13 – the reading is uncertain), but in Mesopotamia Sirius was known as 'the Spear' (*mulkak-si-sá*) and Canis Major as 'the Bow' (*mul ᵍⁱšban*). In the Old Testament the Pleiades are 'the Cluster' (*kîmā*; Job 9.9; 38.31; Amos 5.8), but in Babylonian 'the Mane (of Taurus)' (*mulzappu*) and in Sumerian 'the Stars' (*mul-mul*). Orion in the Old Testament is named 'the Stout One' or 'the Clumsy Fool' (*kᵉsîl*; Job 9.9; 38.31; Amos 5.8), but in Mesopotamia 'the Faithful Shepherd of

Anu' (*mulsipa-zi-an-na*) and in Babylonian texts 'the (Star of the) One Cleft by the Weapon' (*šitaddaru/šitaddalu*, meaning uncertain). On the basis of textual emendation three further star-names are found in Amos 5.9[100] and these possibly bear some similarity to their Babylonian counterparts. Taurus is here called 'the Bull' (*šōr*), Capella 'the Goat' (*'ēz*) and Vindemiator in Virgo 'the Vintager' (*mebaṣṣēr*). In Mesopotamia Taurus was 'the Bull of Heaven' (*mulgud-an-na*); whilst 'the Goat' (*muluza*) seems to have been the name for the constellation Lyra or for part of Capricorn, Capella may have been 'the Ram' (*muludu-nita*); and although no name is known which corresponds to Vindemiator, the constellation Virgo was known as 'the Furrow' (*mulab-sín*) and may therefore also be associated with the season of harvest. However, it may be of greater significance that the Israelite nomenclature in this instance corresponds more closely with that found amongst the Greeks who gave Taurus, Capella and Vindemiator precisely the same names, ταῦρος, αἴξ and προτρυγητήρ.[101] Some further constellations are found in the Old Testament, but these have proved exceedingly difficult to identify. 'The Chamber' (*ḥeder*; Job 37.9) and 'the Chambers of the South' (*ḥadrē tēmān*; Job 9.9) are often thought to be the same group of stars, probably some constellation or region of the southern sky.[102] The *mazzārōt* (Job 38.32) remains a mystery.[103] It has also been suggested that *liwyātān nāḥāš bāriaḥ*, *liwyātān nāḥāš 'aqallātōn* and *hattannīn 'ašer bayyām* in Isa. 27.1 should be identified with Serpens, Draco and Hydra,[104] but it is more likely that these names are of purely mythological reference without astral significance, since similar serpent-names, *ltn*, *btn.brḥ* and *btn. 'qltn*, are known from the Ugaritic texts where they appear to have no connection with the stars whatsoever.[105] Even though there are many problems involved in identifying the Babylonian star-names and despite the equally, if not more confusing uncertainties in the study of the Old Testament astronomical data, it seems that the outline given here is sufficient to show that, wherever the Israelites obtained their astral lore, it was to a significant degree independent of its Mesopotamian counterpart and may indeed well have been largely indigenous to the land of Canaan.

Stars in the Old Testament were animate bodies with names (Ps. 147.4) who ruled over the night (Ps. 136.7–9), who gave praise to Yahweh (Ps. 148.3; Neh. 9.6), who with the sons of God sang at Yahweh's creation (Job. 38.7), and who fought for the Israelites in battle against the Canaanites (Judg. 5.20). Balaam prophesied that Israel's leader should be a 'star out of Jacob and a comet[106] out of Israel' (Num. 24.17), and the captain of Yahweh's host with drawn sword before Jericho may have been just such a comet (Josh. 5.13–14).[107] There can be consequently little doubt that when Micaiah ben Imlah saw Yahweh 'sitting on his throne and all the Host of Heaven standing by him', the heavenly court included astral beings (I Kings 22.19). Micaiah was not a polytheist, however, for the stars were always subject to Yahweh's authority (Job. 9.7; Ps. 147.4; Amos 5.8–9).

Old Testament astral mythology includes an apocalyptic vision of a heavenly battle in which Yahweh emerges victorious over the Host of Heaven. The stars, together with the Sun, the Moon and the rulers of the Earth, are finally imprisoned in the Pit, while Yahweh reigns triumphant from Zion (Isa. 24.21–3; cf. 13.10; 34.4). Presumably there is an element of polemic against the cult of the heavenly bodies in this myth, but it seems impossible to trace any clue which would suggest the provenance or nature of the astral deities in question. Certainly there is no instance in which the myth occurs in an oracle pre-dating the period of Assyrian domination and it may be that the prophet had Assyrian gods in mind, but this is by no means clear. There is, however, a second myth, that of Helel ben Shahar in Isa. 14.12–15, which, although it post-dates the Assyrian period in its present form, shows no trace of Assyrian influence, but belongs indubitably to a cycle of myths associated with the western seaboard.[108] Helel, who is Venus as the morning star, son of the Dawn-goddess, Shahar,[109] attempted to mount above the stars of El (*mimma'al leḳōḳebē-'ēl*) and set his throne on the mount of assembly (*beharmōʿēd*) in the recesses of Ṣaphon (*beyarketē ṣāpōn*) in an attempt to emulate Elyon (*'eddammeh leʿelyōn*). His attempt was unsuccessful and he ended in Sheol, in the Pit (*bōr*). The terminology is thoroughly Canaanite-Palestinian without trace of Mesopotamian influence and the myth may be related to the Greek account of the fall of Phaethon from the chariot of Helios and to the Ugaritic tradition of the failure of Athtar to occupy the throne of the dead Baal. Although the precise identification of Helel and Shahar has been debated, the cultural context of the myth is Greece, Phoenicia and Canaan, and its recurrence in varying versions and in different contexts in Greece, Ugarit and the Old Testament once more points to the conclusion that Israel's astral beliefs were nearer to those of her western neighbours than to those of Mesopotamia, even after the period of Assyrian domination.[110]

Finally, in the Old Testament there is only one passage, Jer. 10.2, which could suggest that the Israelites may have shown any interest in astrology before or during the period of Assyrian rule:[111]

> Learn not the customs of the nations,
>   fear not the signs of heaven,
>   even though the nations stand in fear of them.[112]

Here it could be argued that the word '*ōt* (sign) is cognate with the Accadian *ittu* which is used of ominous signs in Mesopotamian astrology and that these were indeed frequently signs that were to be feared.[113] But it could equally be argued that the 'signs of heaven' to which the prophet referred were extraordinary natural phenomena such as eclipses, comets, meteors, or even awesome meteorological phenomena such as lightning or unusual cloud formations. Whilst such signs were also important to the Assyrian omen readers, there is nothing to indicate that the fear of them in Israel belongs to any other sphere than universal primitive religious apprehension.[114] Several other types of divination are known to have been practised in Israel during the Assyrian period, such as soothsaying by observation of the clouds, divination by snake charming or with the use of arrows, sorcery and necromancy, but none of these suggest an interest in astrology and all of them appear to have been practised in Palestine in earlier times.[115]

In view of the foregoing survey it may now be concluded that solar, lunar and astral religions were familiar to the Israelites in many forms from almost every one of their neighbours and that in Palestine itself they were known and their gods held in veneration from earliest times and during the period of the monarchy.[116] Wherever it has been possible to investigate the nature of the astral bodies that featured in Israelite belief, it has been found that they belong to the Canaanite-Palestinian *milieu*, and it has never been necessary, and frequently impossible, to define them in Mesopotamian terms. Whilst it is very likely that the Host of Heaven included deities which were originally Assyrian importations, it seems illogical to define Judah's star cults solely in terms of

Assyrian gods whose worship was officially required as a symbol of vassal status. 'Host of Heaven' was a Palestinian term for the heavenly court (cf. I Kings 22.19), possibly originating in some similar Canaanite expression, and the Mesopotamians, it appears, never thought of the stars as a host or an army.[117] On the whole, our material and literary evidences indicate that the astral beliefs and associated cultic practices of early Israel were of a popular and superstitious nature, as were the cult of the Queen of Heaven and the various divinatory practices current in the land. But it is the case that some of these cults and practices found their way into the official religious centres of the land during the period of Assyrian domination,[118] and it is largely on the basis of this information alone that these cults have so often been defined as Assyrian. However, it now seems that it would be much more to the point to consider the suggestion that the Israelites, who, before the Assyrian invasion, had their own astral lore and venerated the stars in a fairly popular and superstitious manner, began, in the age of religious licence which started about 734 BC, to allow these indigenous superstitious cults to come to prominence, partly because of Assyrian cultural influence, but largely because of the failure of Yahweh to protect against the might of Ashur.[119]

VII

THE ASSYRIAN RELIGIO-POLITICAL IDEAL

Throughout this study it has constantly been maintained that the Old Testament contains no evidence to support the theory that Judah was under obligation to introduce the cult of Assyrian gods. However, it may still be argued that lack of concrete evidence does not destroy the hypothesis, for, if the Assyrians did commonly impose such religious sanctions on defeated peoples, the likelihood is that Judah also was under obligation to worship the Assyrian gods, whether the Old Testament makes explicit statement to that effect or not. There is, however, no clear evidence that the Assyrians did as a rule make such demands. Assyrian historical sources universally attest the high military status of the god Ashur. He was the Assyrian war-lord to whom all victories and military guidance were accredited. It was he who subjugated and held in submission, while the Assyrian king shared in his glory as his vicegerent and commander in the field. Assyria's expansionist policy had as its goal the subjection of the world to Ashur, as was his right. As a result, all defeated gods and nations were subject and vassal to the overlordship of Ashur.[1] Few scholars would raise objections to any of these statements, since they can be adequately supported from Assyrian writings, but here the question being asked is whether it is legitimate to go one step further and infer that the Assyrians required their vassals to introduce the cult of Ashur to their state sanctuaries.[2]

Gressmann, whilst admitting that further research was needed, maintained that this question should have an affirmative answer. On the basis of a series of texts which show that the Assyrians frequently confiscated the gods of captured towns, he argued that the defeated were deprived of the protection of their deities.[3] Then, noting that Ashurbanipal, when he reconquered Babylon after Shamash-shum-ukin's revolt, commanded the Babylonians to offer 'the former (?), established, regular sacrifices for Ashur, Bêlit (*sic*) and the great gods of Assyria',[4] he concluded that the Assyrians imposed the worship of their gods on the vanquished. However, it is not at all obvious that these texts do support Gressmann's conclusions. Streck, on whom Gressmann relied for his information, noted that the deportation of the gods of conquered peoples was 'in accordance with a widely practised war-custom in the ancient orient'.[5] This indeed seems to be correct, for it is known that defeated gods were deported by the Babylonians,[6] the Elamites,[7] the Philistines[8] and possibly by the Israelites.[9] There is therefore no *a priori* reason for believing that this action on the part of the Assyrians indicates that their religio-political ideal was any different from that of their Near Eastern neighbours. Furthermore, it is also most noteworthy that in each of the texts cited by Streck and referred to by Gressmann the idols are included in lists of booty, the components of which have little or no religious significance. On the contrary, these lists would suggest that the idols were taken, not for religious reasons, but as lucrative spoils of war.[10] And nowhere is it suggested that the confiscated gods were replaced by Assyrian deities.

Nor does the second part of Gressmann's argument carry conviction. It appears that the precise meaning of the text of Ashurbanipal's *Annals* at the particular point to which he referred is open to debate, but a possible translation is 'I imposed upon them regular offerings of the first quality for Ashur, Ninlil and the gods of Assyria'.[11] It is, however, not at all clear that these lines read in context do suggest that the Assyrian king re-imposed the worship of Assyrian gods in Babylon. Ashurbanipal describes how he subdued Babylon and re-imposed the 'Yoke of Ashur' (line 103) on the land. This imposition seems to have been tripartite: the appointment of 'governors and prefects' (line 105), the annual collection of a 'royal tribute and tax' (line 108) and the disputed religious burden (lines 106–7). Since two parts of the Yoke of Ashur appear to have taken the form of fiscal arrangements, it seems more likely that the third part was a demand for financial contribution (possibly in kind) to the Assyrian state religion than a requirement to restore an Assyrian sacrificial cultus in Babylon.

There are many parallels to this imposition in Assyrian records, but nowhere do they give the impression of being more than a demand for tribute to be paid to the state cult.[12] However that may be, it is almost incredible that Ashurbanipal should have attempted to impose the cult of Ashur, Ninlil and the gods of Assyria in Babylon where Marduk reigned supreme, for throughout their history the Assyrians had respected and recognized the supremacy of Marduk in Babylon, even at times regarding him almost as the equal of Ashur.[13] It may hardly be doubted that the new governors of Babylon and other Assyrians resident in Babylon would soon have had their own cult of Ashur and the Assyrian gods in operation again[14] if the cult of these gods had been temporarily discontinued during Shamash-shum-ukin's rebellion, but this would have happened without a formal decree of obligation issued by the king.

It would naturally be expected that, if our question is to be given an affirmative answer, more positive evidence would be found in the Assyrian treaties, but this is not the case. Of course it could be argued that this is due to the fact that we possess relatively few texts of Assyrian treaties and that many of these are fragmentary, but, taken together with the historical texts, their lack of evidence is striking. Notwithstanding, it has sometimes been noted that the Assyrians swore their treaties by their own gods only,[15] but no positive conclusions may be based on this observation, for the treaty between Esarhaddon and Baal of Tyre lists among the gods invoked Bethel, Anat-Bethel, Baal-shamain, Baal-malage, Baal-ṣaphon, Melqart, Eshmun and Astarte,[16] all of them Canaanite-Phoenician deities. This one exception out of three or four extant Assyrian treaties is surely significant for the present investigation.[17] The fragmentary state of some of the other treaties may also be important here; for example, in the treaty between Ashurnirari V and Mati'ilu of Arpad the ending of the curse list is lost.[18] The complete curse list survives in the Vassal Treaty of Esarhaddon (hereinafter VTE) and the gods invoked by name are Assyrian, but since this treaty was made with all Assyria's vassals, it would have been impractical to list all or even a selection of the gods of the many subject peoples. Hence the names of their gods are probably comprehended in such phrases as 'the gods of every land'.[19]

Perhaps the nearest thing in the treaties to the imposition of

Assyrian cults is to be found in VTE. Following immediately upon the stipulations are two paragraphs in which Ashur is named as god of the subject peoples.[20] Unfortunately the text in both instances is fragmentary and the translation is disputed, but a few fairly general observations are possible. VTE is entirely concerned with the appointment of Ashurbanipal as crown prince and with ascertaining the fidelity of Assyrian subjects to him. It is to securing this oath of allegiance that the first paragraph, lines 385–96, is directed. Here the vassal is warned: if you fail to put your whole heart and soul into swearing the oath, if you do not transmit the stipulations to your children, or if you harbour any intention of breaking the treaty, then 'may your sons and grandsons because of this fear in the future, forever, your god Ashur (*aššur* DINGIR-[*ku-nu*]) and your lord, the crown prince designate Ashurbanipal' (lines 393–6).[21] The implication, it seems, is that the vassal, if he refuses to uphold the treaty, has the wrath of his overlords to fear. As Ashurbanipal's own lord is Ashur, the vassal is reminded that he has also submitted to the overlordship of the god of Assyria. This much seems clear, but it is doubtful whether more should be read into the passage in order to support the conclusion that the vassals were required to introduce the cult of Ashur to their native shrines. The treaty demands respect for and submission to the Assyrian royal line and the import of the text is that the sanction for continued fidelity will be the powerful authority of the overlord and his god.[22]

Unfortunately the text of the second paragraph, lines 397–409, is badly damaged,[23] but it appears to be concerned with the protection of the treaty document and the authority of the seals.[24] The vassal is charged not to deface the treaty in any way, but to pay the respect due from him to the persons whose authority is represented on the document by the seals, namely Esarhaddon, Ashur and Ashurbanipal. He is thus reminded that he must 'respect as your own god (DINGIR-*ku-n*[*u*], line 409) Ashur, king of the gods', whose image is on '[the tablet] sealed with the seal of Ashur, king of the gods, and placed before you —'.[25] Therefore, in so far as it is possible to interpret this fragmentary section, it seems that, whilst it is clear that the vassal is reminded of the lordly power and authority of the Assyrian rulers and their god, Ashur, there is no obvious reason why the text should be thought to suggest that he was required to introduce the cult of Ashur to his own capital city.

The vassal is warned that he must not tamper in any way with the copy of the treaty which is set before him. It bears the impress of Ashur and he must show due reverence to him, just as if he were his own god. Likewise, he must respect the seals of Esarhaddon and Ashurbanipal, for all these seals are the signs of imperial authority over him.[26]

In this connection it is of interest to note that similar demands were made on the vassals in the Jerusalem cult, in the context of the hope for the establishment of Davidic world rule from Zion.

> Now then, you kings, be wise;
>   learn your lesson, you judges of the earth.
> Serve Yahweh with fear,
>   and with trembling kiss his feet,[27]
> Lest he be angry, and you are struck down in your travels,
>   for his wrath flares up in no time at all. (Ps. 2.10–12)

The kings and rulers of the nations were required to reverence Yahweh as their overlord and warned to fear his wrath if they failed to live up to the treaty demands, but there is no suggestion in the Old Testament that they were to introduce his cult to their national sanctuaries.

VTE is an example of Assyrian dealings with those who were already living under the Yoke of Ashur[28] and, although the extant copies of the text would appear to suggest that the subjects came from states to the east of Assyria,[29] VTE 9–10 claims that the treaty was made with 'all over whom Esarhaddon exercises kingship and lordship',[30] including, presumably, Judah. In 672 BC, the year in which the treaty was signed,[31] Judah had been vassal for about sixty years and knew well the might and power of Ashur. The texts in question would therefore have meant much to Manasseh, if he was called upon to swear the oath of allegiance,[32] but it is doubtful whether he, or any other vassal, would have interpreted them as demanding the worship of Ashur in his own capital city.

To a certain degree other peoples of the ancient Orient looked on their own chief deity in a manner similar to the Assyrians' attitude to Ashur. Although Mesha of Moab claimed most of the honour of his victories for himself, he acted for and under the guidance of Kemosh. Booty and prisoners were dedicated to Kemosh, and it was the god who instigated the capture of Nebo.[33] Azitawadda of Adana attributed his victories over certain western powers to 'Baal and the gods';[34] Zakir of Hamath and Lu'ath accredited his victories to Baalshamain.[35] It is true that neither Moab nor these northern cities are known to have had imperial aspirations like Assyria, but Israel had, and it was thanks to Yahweh that Israel was able to assert herself against the Canaanites (Judg. 5.4–5), that David took Edom (II Sam. 8.14) and that Israel defeated the Philistines (I Sam. 17.45–7). Yahweh even claimed imperial supremacy over the foes of Israel (Ps. 2.8; 72.8–11; 89.20ff.). Although this claim must at times during Israel's history have seemed more religious and ideal than practical and political, it had none the less been partly realized during the reigns of David and Solomon. Thus, whilst the gods of Moab and the Syro-Phoenician states were war-lords as was Ashur, the God of Israel made claims that were in many respects similar to the imperial claims of the Assyrian god,[36] but it has not been suggested that Moab, the Syro-Phoenician states, or Israel tried to impose the worship of their gods on defeated nations.[37] Likewise, without further information it would be rash to read more into the Assyrian religio-political ideal than a determination to subject the world to Ashur's overlordship.

It cannot be denied that Assyrian religion often followed in the wake of the Assyrian armies and that it was at times adopted officially by a vassal state. Bar-rekub of Zinjirli, for instance, claimed that his 'lord is *b'l* of Haran',[38] but there is no evidence that he was obliged to make that claim. It would, however, be wrong to suggest that the Assyrians never enforced the worship of Ashur on defeated people,[39] but in view of the mass of information now available from Assyrian archives, it is significant that the theory that Assyrian vassals were required to worship Ashur in their state sanctuaries finds so little support in Assyrian records, and that mainly in a particular interpretation of one or two isolated texts which are probably best explained in some other way. The various aspects of the Assyrian religio-political ideal to which appeal has been or may be made are not of the sort that lend weight to a theory of enforced religion in the empire. For example, it is of little consequence to our conclusions whether Assyrian gods were occasionally worshipped by subject races, for their presence may signify nothing more than cultural diffusion. It is also immaterial whether some symbol of Assyrian overlordship, such as a treaty document, had to be placed in the vassal's shrine, for such objects do not require to be worshipped. Again, statements to the effect that the victor's god is more powerful than the god of the vanquished do not imply the imposition of worship. Similarly, a requirement to recognize the victor's god as overlord cannot prove the obligatory worship of that god. What is sought is some statement or suggestion that the vassal was required to institute in his native shrine an official cult to the god of the Assyrian overlord, and furthermore some indication that such was or may have been common Assyrian practice. The records of the Assyrians do indeed provide much information relating to their religio-political ideal, but rather significantly they lack the evidence required to show that it included such a requirement as a regular feature of some importance.[40]

VIII

CONCLUSIONS

For several decades now the theory that the Assyrians imposed the worship of their gods on Judah has been widely accepted and has formed the basis for many detailed studies in Old Testament history and religion. But in the preceding chapters an attempt has been made to show that this hypothesis rests on an unsubstantial foundation. The various deities worshipped in Judah during the period of Assyrian domination lack the definitive aspects of the Assyrian gods and generally exhibit the characteristics of popular Palestinian paganism. Furthermore, many of the deities hitherto regarded as Assyrian, for example, the Queen of Heaven, were worshipped, not as official representatives of the overlord in the Temple, but in the local cults of the Judaean populace. In like manner, it has been seen that the cultic innovations of Ahaz and Manasseh, heretofore interpreted in terms of the overlord's imposition of religious sanctions, do not appear to have been acts of Assyrianization, but rather to reflect many different forms of digression from traditional Yahwism and apostasy to a wide variety of indigenous and foreign practices. Similarly, in the accounts of the purges of Hezekiah and Josiah no element of anti-Assyrian polemic has been found and it seems logical to infer that Assyrian cults played no significant part in the politics or the religion of Judah. This conclusion, it has been seen, is further supported by the observation that extant Near Eastern writings offer no evidence to support the thesis that imposition of the cult of Ashur was a regular feature of any importance in the Assyrian religio-political ideal.

On the other hand, it is not suggested that there was no

Assyrian religious influence in this period. Indeed, the Old Testament clearly indicates that a number of Mesopotamian gods were known and worshipped in Judah both before and after the time of the nation's vassaldom. But there is no indication whatsoever that these represented an official Assyrian presence in the land.

Many commentators have argued that mention of the names Sakkuth and Kaiwan is made in Amos 5.26, although not all would agree with the emendation required to sustain this reading.[1] But if this verse did originally contain these names, then it provides evidence for the presence of Mesopotamian gods, possibly both astral, in Israel. *Sak-kud* is the name of a deity equated in a Babylonian god-list with Ninurta who had a secondary association with the planet Saturn,[2] and in Accadian sources Saturn was sometimes known by the name *kajamānu*, the cognates of which in other Semitic languages are also recognized as the name of the planet Saturn.[3] However, unless this oracle does not derive from the time of Amos himself and has been inserted by an editor,[4] these gods were already in Palestine before the time of Tiglath-pileser's campaigns in the west. But even if the verse were from the pen of a later writer, it would still have to be shown that the Israelites were under obligation to worship these gods and there is nothing in the text, uncertain as its true meaning may be, that would suggest such a conclusion.

Again, amongst the various other heathen practices enumerated in Ezek. 8,[5] vv. 14–15 tell of a ritual in which women were weeping for Tammuz. It is difficult to decide when this and the other abuses described would first have been introduced and it is likely that some of the cults pre-date Josiah in origin and were revived after his death, but the whole chapter as it now stands seems to give a picture of paganism in Jerusalem after 597 BC, that is, sometime after the fall of Assyria and certainly well after Josiah's reforms.[6] Tammuz (Sumerian and Babylonian *Dumu-zi*), a dying and rising vegetation god, was well known from Sumerian times and his cult was one of the most popular in Mesopotamia. It could therefore well have spread to Palestine during the period of Assyrian domination and may be the cult mentioned in Isa. 17.10–11,[7] but it seems highly unlikely that the Assyrians would have required their Judaean subjects to serve Tammuz as a sign of vassal status, for he was, after all, more a Babylonian than an Assyrian god – and is therefore more likely to have entered Jerusalem under Babylonian influence.

After the fall of Samaria in 722 BC, the peoples who were re-settled in the land brought with them gods from Mesopotamia and elsewhere (II Kings 17.30–1). Men from Babylon brought Sukkoth-benoth, whose identity is debated,[8] but who was doubt-less of Mesopotamian origin. Settlers from Cuth (modern *Tell Ibrāhīm*, to the north of Babylon) took with them Nergal, the Mesopotamian god of the underworld, god of death, pestilence and fire, who was associated with the planet Mars.[9] From Hamath on the Orontes came the Syrian god, Ashima,[10] from Awwa the Elamite gods Nibhaz and Tartak,[11] and from Sepharvaim the composite gods Adrammelech and Anammelech.[12] Several of these can be regarded as Mesopotamian deities with astral asso-ciations of some kind, and they may even have become members of the Israelite Host of Heaven after a time. But their worship was brought to northern Israel by settlers and was not imposed on the old population by imperial decree.

There can now be little doubt that Mesopotamian gods were worshipped in Judah after 732 BC. It would indeed be surprising if it had been otherwise. This was the age of Assyrian domination when mass folk-movement, land resettlement and military up-heaval promoted international intercourse. Hence the gods mocked by Amos, if they were in the land before 732 BC, were probably first brought by traders and settlers. In the same way, as Assyrian trading and military involvement in Judah increased, so there must have been a corresponding increase of Mesopotamian religion. Furthermore, since it was only fifteen miles from Bethel to Jerusalem, the upsurge of Mesopotamian heathenism in the North must have resulted in its infiltration into Judah, particu-larly during the reign of Manasseh. Hence Ezekiel upbraided Judah because she played the harlot, not only with Egypt, Canaan and Babylon, but also with Assyria (Ezek. 16.23–9; 23.11–21). Nonetheless, it is perhaps significant (albeit unfortunate) that we possess the name of no Mesopotamian deity worshipped in Judah during the age of Assyrian rule, for it has been seen throughout this study that there is nothing in the Old Testament to distin-guish the status of Assyrian religion from the many other pagan cults in the land at this time. On the basis of the evidence avail-able it could even be thought that the Old Testament silence about

Assyrian cults in this age should signify that they were not as important as marks of apostasy as the indigenous paganism of Canaan.

If these conclusions are correct, then several aspects of Judah's history stand in need of reassessment. For example, if Ahaz and Manasseh did not pursue a rigorous policy of Assyrianizing the Jerusalem cult and if the reforms of Hezekiah and Josiah were not first and foremost acts of rebellion, there is perhaps more scope for an understanding of Israelite history in which religious zeal played a formative role. It may be possible to think of other pressures and influences operative in effecting the various changes which took place, for the determinative factors in the history of a period of over a hundred years must have been many. A detailed investigation of such possibilities is clearly beyond the scope of the present work, but indications have been given throughout of the direction in which such enquiry may lead. Let it therefore suffice that these tentative suggestions be here summarized, not as proven conclusions, but as proposals for future evaluation.[13]

The action of Ahaz in calling upon Tiglath-pileser III for help was based on fear and lack of confidence in the ability of Yahweh to protect and the nation to withstand in the face of aggression. In consequence Judah sank to the status of vassaldom. These conditions were ideally suited for apostasy, not only amongst the people, but also in the national sanctuary. To meet the heavy cost of tribute to Assyria, the rich cultic apparatus of the Temple was plundered, whilst the altar of burnt sacrifices, hallowed by age and tradition, was now replaced by a copy of a Syrian altar, perhaps the one on which Ahaz had ratified the treaty with Tiglath-pileser. Further altars were erected on the roof-tops, probably for the worship of astral gods, and the decay of religion, thus aggravated by the superstition and faithlessness of Ahaz, rapidly affected the people who now more and more turned to Baalism and even instituted the deplorable rites of the Hinnom Valley. It was an age of national decline when the religious hopes of the people were gradually undermined and eroded. Assyrian armies were on the threshold and the sister kingdom in the north was being destroyed before their very eyes. In such times, particularly if the leadership is not strong, superstitious and pagan rites based on fear come naturally to the surface. Thus we find that under Ahaz, when 'his heart and the heart of his people shook as the trees of the forest shake before the wind' (Isa. 7.2), Yahweh was increasingly forsaken for the false hope that comes from empty cult and dark ritual.

Under Hezekiah a glimmer of hope returned. Judah, with various other Palestinian states, rebelled against Assyria in the sincere hope that independence could be re-established. The nationalistic zeal engendered on this occasion was sufficient to encourage both king and people to rally to the banner of their god and put their whole trust in his power to save. Naturally this meant that the cult had to be purged, strengthened and unified, and so we read that Hezekiah carried out a set of reforms, but doubtless there were also other influences operative at this time. The preaching of Micah and Isaiah, and possibly of early Deuteronomists, was no longer falling on deaf ears, for king and people were for a time prepared to listen to their call to support the national god. Yahweh was therefore declared sovereign and independent, and all symbols of his vassal status were removed. A 'miraculous' deliverance of the city from the jaws of the powerful Assyrian army added further impetus to this zeal and must indubitably have encouraged further reforming activity throughout the land.

However, the excitement and religious fervour were short-lived. Judah was not strong enough to maintain her independent status and now entered a long 'dark age' of vassaldom which continued more or less unbroken for well over half the seventh century. Once more true Yahwism went into partial eclipse behind the resurgent paganism of Ahaz's reign. The Canaanite cults reappeared throughout the land and the obnoxious rites in honour of Molech were revived. Astral cults flourished together with such superstitious practices as divination and necromancy. Yahwistic zeal had dwindled with the departure of hope for independence and its decline amongst the populace was given additional impetus by the example set by the king himself. Manasseh, probably because of his marriages and other alliances, introduced the Phoenician cults of Baal and Asherah to the national shrine itself and dedicated a plot of land in the city to the god of his Arabian wife. The stars were also venerated in the Temple, no doubt partly as a result of Assyrian influence, and a Sun-cult with horses and chariots and with its own sacred buildings was established in the Temple court. These and other abuses illustrate the multiform nature of paganism under Manasseh, and doubtless behind each non-Yahwistic cult and practice there lies a tale that can no longer be told. But the complexity itself is an indication that no one, simple hypothesis will solve all the mysteries of this obscure period. To be sure, Assyrian influence must have been considerable by this time, but it seems that Manasseh's sympathies were not undivided. The Assyrian king, if the Chronicler's tradition is to be valued, did not always think that Manasseh's fidelity was beyond question, and it may be that his grounds for suspicion lay in the observation that Manasseh maintained close contact with his neighbours, who were not the least troublesome of Assyrian vassals. These unions and alliances have left their traces on the accounts of his reign, as also have a whole variety of other pressures and circumstances, many of which are now inevitably lost to history.

After the death of Manasseh, Judah began to reawaken to the possibility of rebellion. Unfortunately we do not know the reasons for Amon's assassination, but it may be surmised that it was a symptom of this renascent spirit, for the party which put Josiah on the throne did lead the country to both independence and reform. How the rebellion and the reformation were interrelated is now difficult to determine, since the Old Testament has preserved no record of the former. But it is likely that, as in the days of Hezekiah, resurgent nationalism contributed much to the demand for cultic purity and unity centred on the worship of the God of Israel. Again, as in the days of Hezekiah, religious zeal was stirred by prophets (Zephaniah and Jeremiah) and also by the Deuteronomists. Although *Urdeuteronomium* was not publicly produced until the eighteenth year of Josiah's reign, its proponents must have been active for some time before that date, probably even in the royal court itself. As their work and teaching both encouraged and was concurrent with the revival of Yahwistic zeal, they were able to apply their energies to guiding the reforms on a more positive course than mere iconoclasm. Doubtless any Assyrian gods in the Temple and the land would have been swept away, but only as an act of reformation, not as a declaration of rebellion. Political factors were indeed important. They set the tenor of the age. But they did not dictate the course of the reformation. This was controlled by something much deeper; by the zeal for Yahweh which, having lain dormant in the hearts of many, now burst into flame when the voice of God was heard once more in the land calling all true Israelites to his service.

> And now, O Israel, what does Yahweh your God require from you? Only to fear Yahweh your God, to walk in all his ways and to love him; to serve Yahweh your God with all your heart and all your being; to keep the commandments of Yahweh and his statutes . . . (Deut. 10.12–13)

POSTSCRIPT

In my discussions with other scholars, three arguments have frequently been put forward. Firstly, it has been suggested to me that I am attempting to separate politics and religion as no ancient Semite could have done. When Judah submitted to Assyria, Ashur would inevitably have entered the Temple in Jerusalem; this is just how the ancient mind worked. I do not find this argument convincing. It implies, for example, that those left in Judah after 597 BC worshipped Marduk, that the restored community in Jerusalem after 540 BC worshipped Ahuramazda, and that the peoples of Edom, Moab and Damascus worshipped Yahweh under David and Solomon, but our sources suggest that, in these cases at least, politics and religion were by no means so inseparable in the ancient world that the gods of the overlord did of necessity follow his armies. Certainly politics and religion were intimately connected, but the religio-political ideal of the ancient Semites was not therefore identical to that of the later Greeks and Romans who did try to impose or encourage the worship of their gods throughout their empires.

Secondly, it has been argued that there must be more than just coincidence in the facts that the rebel kings were the ones who attempted to reform the cult, that the reigns of the subservient kings were marked by unbroken apostasy, and that the Host of Heaven was worshipped only during the age of Assyrian domination. This is a good argument, but it cannot be conclusive, for it is possible to interpret the 'coincidence' in different ways. Although the Old Testament does not refer to a cult of the Host of Heaven before the Assyrian era, there is no reason to think that the stars were not worshipped at a popular level in earlier times. (Indeed, very little is known of Judaean paganism before the mid-eighth century.) The upsurge of this and other kinds of paganism may come naturally at a time when Yahweh had been shown to be weak and it is probably equally natural that reforming fervour should rise to the surface in times of hope for future liberation. No imperial edict is needed to govern such movements in a people's religion.

The third argument, and the weakest, which has been presented to me, is that the theory of religious sanctions imposed by the Assyrians is a working hypothesis which does give a coherent solution to many of the *cruces interpretatum* of Judaean history. But 'working hypothesis' is not coterminous with 'historical truth' (as far as that can be determined), and any such hypothesis must be abandoned, even in favour of no alternative, if the material evidence to support it is lacking or points in another direction.

It has also been urged that in admitting the likelihood of Assyrian influence through gradual infiltration of religious ideas and practices I have all but surrendered to my oponents. Again I cannot agree, for history is not a study in black and white, but a portrait painted in many shades and colours. I should therefore not wish to deny totally the value of the first two of the above arguments, for there are doubtless shades of truth in each of them. The political status of Judah did probably contribute much to the rise of Assyrian religion in the land and indubitably the events of Judaean history were governed by more than mere coincidence, but neither of these observations necessitates an interpretation in terms of official religious sanctions.

NOTES

CHAPTER I

1. Th. Östreicher, *Das deuteronomische Grundgesetz*, Beiträge zur Förderung christlicher Theologie 27.4, Gütersloh 1923.

2. *Ibid.*, pp.9–10; but see my comments on p. 74f.

3. *Ibid.*, p.38; but see my discussion in ch.II.

4. *Ibid.*, p.69; on the problem of chronology see E. W. Nicholson, *Deuteronomy and Tradition*, Oxford 1967, pp.10–11.

5. *Ibid.*, p.40. His argument that the reforms began in Josiah's twelfth year, before the finding of the law-book, is based on the information given in II Chron. 34.3ff. (*ibid.*, p.64), and has been widely accepted; see E. W. Nicholson, *op. cit.*, p.9, n.6 and bibliography given there.

6. *Ibid.*, pp.41ff. Here his analysis mainly follows the order of events as set forth in II Kings 23.4–14. But some scholars would argue that these verses may derive from more than one source; see p.3 and ch.V, n.5.

7. *Ibid.*, p.41; but on this verse see my remarks on p.3 of.

8. *Ibid.*, p.42; but see pp.36–9 of this book.

9. *Ibid.*, p.43.

10. *Ibid.*, pp.43–50; but see ch.III, n.41.

11. *Ibid.*, pp.53–5; but see my discussion on pp.32–6 and ch.III, n.27.

12. *Ibid.*, pp.55–6.

13. It seems unnecessary to give a bibliographic account of the extent of Östreicher's influence, for almost every book or article dealing with this period written since 1923 shows acceptance of his thesis, albeit frequently with modifications. In the course of the chapters that follow reference is limited for the most part to works which have made some kind of contribution to the debate. The present climate of opinion is neatly outlined by E. W. Nicholson, *op. cit.*, pp.9ff.; cf. G. Fohrer, *Introduction to the Old Testament*, ET, London 1970, p. 168.

14. O. Procksch, 'König Josia', *Festgabe für Theodor Zahn*, Leipzig 1928, pp.19–53. Some of his arguments are criticized by A. Jepsen, 'Die Reform des Josia', *Festschrift Friedrich Baumgärtel zum 70. Geburtstag*, ed. J. Herrmann, Erlangener Forschungen A:10, Erlangen 1959, pp.97–108.

15. Jepsen, *art. cit.*

16. E. Sellin, *Geschichte des israelitischen-jüdischen Volkes* I, Leipzig 1924, p.287.

17. F. M. Cross and D. N. Freedman, 'Josiah's Revolt against Assyria', *JNES* 12, 1953, pp.56–8. For criticism, see Nicholson, *op. cit.*, pp.10–11.

18. H. Gressmann, 'Josia und das Deuteronomium', *ZAW* 42, 1924, pp. 313–37. But see pp. 30ff. 60ff.

19. A. T. Olmstead, *History of Palestine and Syria to the Macedonian Conquest*, New York—London 1931, p. 452.

20. See particularly chs. V and VI.

21. See chs. II and IV.

22. G. von Rad, *Deuteronomy, a commentary*, ET, OTL, 1966, pp. 23ff.; *idem*, *Studies in Deuteronomy*, ET, SBT 9, 1953, pp. 6off. But see Nicholson, *op. cit.*, pp. 83ff.; C. Brekelmans, 'Le ḥerem chez les prophètes du royaume du nord et dans le Deutéronome', Bibliotheca Ephemeridum Theologicarum Lovaniensium 12–13.i, Paris 1959, pp. 377–83.

23. The present state of opinion about this aspect of the discussion is described by E. W. Nicholson, *op. cit.*, pp. 9ff.

24. So de Vaux, Parrot, Heaton, Ackroyd, Saggs; see ch. II, nn. 9, 10, 20.

25. So, for example, Rudolph, Bright, Myers; see ch. IV, n. 50 (contrast W. O. E. Oesterley and T. H. Robinson, *A History of Israel* I, Oxford 1932, p. 400; M. Noth, *The History of Israel*, second English edition, London 1960, p. 272). Cf. also Weinfeld and Frankena; see ch. VII, n. 32.

26. See especially ch. V, and particularly the comments by J. A. Montgomery and H. S. Gehman, *A Critical and Exegetical Commentary on the Books of Kings*, ICC, 1950, pp. 456–541, and A. Jepsen, *art. cit.*, pp. 100–1. Both these scholars, however, continue to assert that there was a strong Assyrian religious presence in Judah at this time.

27. A. Caquot; see pp. 50, 59, and ch. VI, nn. 58, 117.

28. H. W. F. Saggs; see ch. VII, nn. 39, 40.

CHAPTER II

1. For an alternative interpretation of these events, see B. Oded, 'The Historical Background of the Syro-Ephraimite War Reconsidered', *CBQ* 34, 1972, pp. 153–65. He argues that the Syro-Ephraimite War must be understood in terms of Damascene expansionist activities.

2. The formula used in II Kings 16.7 is 'I am your slave and your son'. The term '*abdᵉkā* immediately suggests vassal status. Furthermore, D. J. McCarthy, 'Notes on the Love of God in Deuteronomy and the Father-Son Relationship between Yahweh and Israel', *CBQ* 27, 1965, pp. 144–7, has argued that father-son language in the Old Testament often belongs to the vocabulary of Israelite treaty terminology.

3. Östreicher, *op. cit.*, p. 38; Gressmann, *art. cit.*, p. 324; Olmstead, *op. cit.*, p. 452; Oesterley and Robinson, *History* I, p. 377; Montgomery, *Kings*, p. 460; J. Bright, *A History of Israel*², OTL, 1972, pp. 274–5; L. Rost, *Das kleine Credo und andere Studien zum Alten Testament*, Heidelberg 1965, p. 20; J. Gray, *I & II Kings, a commentary*², OTL, 1970, p. 635; H. H. Rowley, 'Hezekiah's Reform and Rebellion', *BJRL* 44, 1962, pp. 395–431, ref. p. 425 (now in his *Men of God. Studies in Old Testament History and Prophecy*, London 1963, pp. 98–132).

4. *ANET*, p.282: '[I received] the tribute of . . . Jehoahaz (*Ia-ú-ḫa-zi*) of Judah (*Ia-ú-da-a-a*) . . .'

5. It seems improbable that Rezin of Damascus would have been as free at this time as II Kings 16.6 implies to lead a foray against the southernmost city of Judah and it is more likely that Edom took advantage of the situation to regain its independence from Judah and seek further territory for itself. Thus in II Kings 16.6 the reading '*ªrām* is probably an error for '*ᵉdōm*, and *rᵉṣîn* a subsequent scribal addition. So most commentators; cf. BH³, RSV, NEB; see Gray, *Kings*, p.632.

6. The Philistine cities probably rose in rebellion against Judah to whom they had been subject since the days of Uzziah (II Chron. 26.6). On the historical value of this record, see W. Rudolph, *Chronikbücher*, HAT 1.21, 1955, p.291; J. M. Myers, *Chronicles* II, AB 13, 1965, p.163; J. Gray, 'The Period and Office of the Prophet Isaiah in the Light of a New Assyrian Tablet', *ExpT* 63, 1952, pp.263–5.

7. This passage is so heavily laden with the Chronicler's theology that it must be treated with great caution in the search for historical information. But if Ahaz and his people were terrified at the approach of the Syro-Ephraimite armies (Isa. 7.2, 4), then it is highly probable that many of Judah's villages had fallen and that fighting men had been slain.

8. For example, the words 'and it was of no help to him' in v.21 are probably to be understood as a corrective to II Kings 16.9.

9. R. de Vaux, *Les livres des rois*, La sainte Bible traduite en Français sous la direction de l'École biblique de Jérusalem, Paris 1958, p.196; cf. his *Ancient Israel, its life and institutions*², ET, London 1965, p.410. See also A. Parrot, *Nineveh and the Old Testament*, Studies in Biblical Archaeology 3, London 1955, p.41, n.1; E. W. Heaton, *The Hebrew Kingdoms*, NCB: OT III, 1968, p.103; A. Šanda, *Die Bücher der Könige* II, EHAT 9, 1912, p.201.

10. E. Dhorme, *Les religions de Babylonie et d'Assyrie*, 'Mana': introduction à l'histoire des religions. 1, Les anciennes religions orientales, 2, Paris 1945, pp.189–90; A. L. Oppenheim, *Ancient Mesopotamia, portrait of a dead civilization*, Chicago and London 1964, pp.191–2. This argument is also used by H. W. F. Saggs, *Assyriology and the Study of the Old Testament*, An inaugural lecture delivered at University College, Cardiff, 1968, Cardiff 1969, pp.21–2, to support the conclusion that the altar of Ahaz was not Assyrian. For illustrations of Assyrian altars, see H. Gressmann, *Altorientalische Bilder zum Alten Testament*², Berlin and Leipzig 1927, figs.439–41, 480, 533–5; and for discussion of their use, see de Vaux, *Ancient Israel*, pp.433–5. W. G. Lambert of the University of Birmingham has written to me on this subject as follows: 'I have discussed this with J. J. Orchard, our Mesopotamian archaeologist here, and we agree that the word ("altar") is unfortunate as used of ancient Mesopotamia. There is really nothing that can usefully be so called. On the one hand there were stands on which incense was burnt, but portable things for the same purpose existed. Then on the other hand there were offering tables, on which food for the gods' meals was put, but these were just like tables today, and could be made e.g. of reeds, since no preparation of food or drink took place on them.'

11. Rost, *op. cit.*, p.20.

12. Olmstead, *op. cit.*, p. 452; cf. Östreicher, *op. cit.*, p. 38: 'There can be no doubt at all that the new altar has to mean the new god, the god of the overlord in Nineveh. . . . the state cult in Jerusalem has become Assyrian. *Cuius regio, eius religio*.'

13. E.g., II Kings 17.24–8 tells of the restoration of one (or more, as the plural verbs in v. 27 may suggest) of the exiled Yahweh priests to revive the cult of the offended local deity, for the new settlers did not know the custom of the god of the land. Likewise, it seems that a Phoenician priest was re-quired for the worship of the Sidonian Baal during the abortive reign of Athaliah, daughter of Ahab and the Sidonian Jezebel (II Kings 11.18). This is suggested by the priest's name, Mattan, which at this period seems to have been Phoenician. The form *mattān* in personal names first appears in Judah in the last days of the kingdom (II Kings 24.17; Jer. 38.1; cf. Lachish Ostracon I, see O. Tufnell, *Lachish III [Tell ed-Duweir]: The Iron Age, with contributions by M. A. Murray and D. Diringer*, The Wellcome-Marston Archaeological Research Expedition to the Near East Publications 3 (text), London—New York—Toronto 1953, p. 331). Otherwise it occurs only in writings of the exilic and post-exilic periods. Outside the Old Testament it is also generally restricted to late writings, being found in the Elephantine papyri (cf. A. Vincent, *La religion des judéo-Araméens d'Éléphantine*, Paris 1937, p. 407) and in Canaanite inscriptions of the second and first centuries BC (cf. *KAI* III, p. 50 and references there). Only two occurrences are known in the eighth century. Tiglath-pileser III mentions a king of Tyre named *Mitenna* and various kings of Arvad were named *Matan-Baʿal* from the ninth century onwards (cf. K. Tallqvist, *Assyrian Personal Names*, Acta Societatis Scientiarum Fennicae 43.1, Helsinki 1914, pp. 138, 135). Thus it would seem that in the time of Athaliah Mattan was primarily a Phoenician name.

14. Isa. 8.2. Of course it is possible to argue that Uriah as a court official would have had to accept any royal edict, even if it meant that he had to become priest to a strange god.

15. There has been some disagreement amongst scholars over the identi-fication of the new altar in II Kings 16.14–15. W. R. Smith, *Lectures on the Religion of the Semites, First Series: The Fundamental Institutions*[2], London 1907, pp. 485–9; J. Skinner, *I & II Kings*, CB, *c.* 1893, pp. 370–1, maintain that it was the bronze altar, but de Vaux, *Rois*, p. 197; Montgomery, *Kings*, p. 460; Gray, *Kings*, p. 636, believe that it was the great altar. Verses 10–13 refer to the new altar simply as *hammizbēaḥ*, but v. 14 opens with the anomalous construction *weʾēt hammizbaḥ hanneḥōšet* (but for parallels to this construction, see Mont-gomery, *Kings*, p. 463), apparently introducing a bronze altar, and in v. 15 *mizbaḥ hanneḥōšet* is distinguished from *hammizbēaḥ haggādōl*. There is a strong tradition that the altars in the tabernacle (Ex. 35.16; 38.2) and in Solomon's Temple (I Kings 8.64; II Chron. 1.5–6; Ezek. 9.2) were of bronze and despite the fact that there is no mention of an altar in the list of Hiram's bronze work (I Kings 7.15–46), it seems reasonable to assume that the new altar was not the *mizbaḥ hanneḥōšet*. This is certainly the most natural understanding of the text and those who claim that the new altar was the bronze one are compelled to conclude that the reference to a bronze altar in I Kings 8.64 is intrusive. There is also a syntactical difficulty in vv. 14–15, but most commentators

accept the MT and emend only *hammizbaḥ* at the beginning of v. 14 to *mizbaḥ*. The resulting sentence contains a predicate introduced by *wāw*-consecutive following an accusative *pendens* (further examples of this construction may be found in I Kings 12.17; 15.13; cf. S. R. Driver, *A Treatise on the Use of the Tenses in Hebrew*[3], Oxford 1892, §127a) and may therefore be translated: 'And the bronze altar which was before Yahweh he brought (it) from before the House, from between the (new) altar and the House of Yahweh, and put it on the north side of the (new) altar'. This interpretation indicates that the old bronze altar was moved from between the new great altar and the Temple and reserved for the king's own private use, while the new altar was to be used by the priest in the daily worship of Yahweh (so *contra* W. F. Albright, *Archaeology and the Religion of Israel*[3], The Ayer Lectures of the Colgate-Rochester Divinity School, 1941, Baltimore 1953, pp. 161–2, who maintains that it was the new altar which was moved to the side for Ahaz's use, since not even the king himself could authorize the removal of the old altar which was protected by sanctity and tradition). It therefore seems most reasonable to interpret the text as suggesting that the new altar was erected permanently before the Temple and consecrated to the use of the service of Yahweh with the ritual described in vv. 12–13, whilst the old bronze altar was removed to the north side. There is, however, a second possible solution to the textual difficulty in v. 14. It is possible to omit *we'ēt hammizbaḥ* with LXX and read v. 14 as the continuation of the sentence in v. 13. If *wayyaqrēb* is then emended to *wayyiqrab* (not supported in the Versions), a mere blood ritual is described and neither altar was moved (' . . . and sprinkled the blood . . . upon the altar of brass which was before Yahweh; and drew near from before the House, between the (new) altar and the House of Yahweh, and applied it (the blood) to the north side of the (new) altar.' So W. R. Smith, *loc. cit.*; J. Skinner, *loc. cit.*). According to this interpretation also the new altar stood before the Temple of Yahweh to be used by Yahweh's priest.

16. As maintained by Šanda, *Könige* II, p. 201; Skinner, *Kings*, pp. 369–70.

17. Šanda, *Könige* II, p. 207; R. Kittel, *Die Bücher der Könige*, HKAT 1.5, 1900, p. 270.

18. If it were still to be assumed that the altar was a copy of an Assyrian prototype, although this now seems virtually impossible, then it is possible to argue, as did some older scholars, that it was introduced to the Temple on the initiative of Ahaz himself who 'saw the Assyrian chief altar in Damascus, and thought he would gain the favour of the great king by imitating it' (R. Kittel, *The History of the Hebrews* II, Theological Translation Library 4, London 1895, p. 348).

19. See Bright, *History*, p. 276.

20. Saggs, *op. cit.*, pp. 21–2. Discussing the nature of the literary sources, P. R. Ackroyd, 'Historians and Prophets', *Svensk Exegetisk Årsbok* 33, 1968, pp. 18–54, suggests (p. 36, n. 21) 'we might ask whether it is the Chronicler's presentation which reinterprets in terms of Damascus, or 2 Kings 16 which offers an interpretation in terms of Assyria.' He also suggests that the changes in the Temple might originally have been unrelated to the Syro-Ephraimite War and were described in their present setting to show how apostate Ahaz was.

21. The first suggestion implies that a major change in the worship of the Temple, the removal of an altar hallowed by centuries of use, was made simply for the sake of trade. Whilst it seems to me improbable, it is not beyond the bounds of possibility that Ahaz with a heavy burden of tribute to bear did not hesitate to take such drastic measures to promote better trading relations.

22. On the same principle the gods of the vassal were included in the curse list of the treaty between Esarhaddon and Baal of Tyre; see p.62. It could also be argued on this hypothesis that the new altar was a symbol of the treaty in much the same way as was the copy of the treaty document which Ahaz would have had to place in the Temple (cf. de Vaux, *Ancient Israel*, p.301).

23. E.g., I. Benzinger, *Die Bücher der Könige*, KHC 9, Freiburg 1899, p.171, and R. Kittel, *Könige*, p.271: 'to ponder over' (what to do with it); cf. Vg: *erit paratum ad voluntatem meam*. J. Morgenstern, *The Fire upon the Altar*, Leiden 1963, p.36: 'to officiate at dawn' (at the New Year Festival); cf. LXX: ἔσται μοι εἰς τὸ πρωί.

24. Although this meaning is not attested elsewhere in the Old Testament, the *Pi'ēl* of *bqr* does have the meaning 'to examine', 'to divide', 'to distinguish'; e.g. in Lev. 13.36 it means 'to examine', in Lev. 27.33 'to discriminate' (between good and evil) and in Rabbinic Hebrew 'to investigate for omens'; cf. Arabic *baqara*, 'to split, rip open'. Hence in II Kings 16.15 it is taken to designate an act of cutting open the sacrificial victim in search of omens. In an astrological text from Ras Shamra (*UT* 143.5) *bqr* is used possibly of divination. See further Gray, *Kings*, p.637.

25. Montgomery, *Kings*, p.461.

26. Gray, *Kings*, p.637. For an example from Gezer, see R. A. S. Macalister, *The Excavation of Gezer.*, *1902–1905 and 1907–1909* II, London 1912, p.454, fig.535, and from Hazor, see Y. Yadin and others, *Hazor III–IV. An account of the third and fourth seasons of excavations*, 1957–1958, The James A. de Rothschild Expedition at Hazor, Jerusalem, 1961, pl. CCCXV (= *ANEP*, pl. 844). See below, fig. 1. The Hazor livers apparently date from the sixteenth century BC and they bear Accadian cuneiform inscriptions (see Y. Yadin, *Hazor, the Head of all those Kingdoms, Joshua 11:10*, Schweich Lectures 1970, London 1972, pp.82–3). But whilst they do not therefore attest to the indigenous practice of omen sacrifice, they are at least evidence that this method of obtaining oracles was introduced to Palestine at a very early date.

27. See above, n.10.

28. Ps.27.4; cf. H. Ringgren, *The Faith of the Psalmists*, London 1963, p.3.

29. Olmstead, *History of Palestine and Syria*, p.452.

30. A. Parrot, *The Temple of Jerusalem*, Studies in Biblical Archaeology 5, London 1955, pp.46–7.

31. So most commentators. Montgomery, *Kings*, p.462, and Skinner, *Kings*, p.372, following Šanda, suggest that *mippᵉnē melek 'aššūr* (v.18) should therefore be read after v.17.

32. *Mûsak haššabbāt* (so *Qᵉrē*). There is little agreement amongst either versions or commentators as to the nature of this structure which in all probability was used in the special Sabbath rituals of the time (cf. also Ezek. 46.1), that is if we are not to point *haššebet* following LXX and think of some

kind of covering for a throne in the Temple. See further Montgomery, *Kings*, pp. 462, 464.

33. *Mᵉbō' hammelek haḥiṣōnā*: 'the king's entrance outwards'. Some commentators prefer to read *haḥiṣōn* and translate 'the outer gate for the king' (NEB). See Montgomery, *ad loc.*

34. *Bēt YHWH* without a preposition, suggesting accusative of direction: 'towards the Temple'. But many commentators suspect that the text is corrupt at this point and that a preposition should be supplied, reading either *bᵉbēt* or *mibbēt*, depending on whether the structures were turned round or removed. Others suggest that the phrase should be omitted altogether. See Montgomery, *Kings, ad loc.*

35. Olmstead, *loc. cit.*

36. The temples in which statues or stelae of Assyrian kings are known to have been placed are all Assyrian. Statues of Esarhaddon and Ashurbanipal were erected in the cult room of Ashur, the *Eḫursagkurkurra*, in Assur, cf. E. F. Weidner, 'Assurbânipal in Assur', *AfO* 13, 1939–41, pp. 204–18, ref. p. 204. A stele of Ashurnasirpal II stood at the entrance to the Ninurta temple at Nimrud. A stele of Adad-nirari III was found inside the cella of the late Assyrian shrine at *Tell al Rimah*. Otherwise stelae of Assyrian kings appear to have been found in settings other than temples or were excavated in such a way that their original context is obscure. See S. Page, 'A Stela of Adad-nirari III and Nergal-ereš from Tell al Rimah', *Iraq* 30, 1968, pp. 139–53, ref. p. 139, n. 1. It may, however, be possible to explain the absence of similar statues from non-Assyrian sanctuaries by the supposition that they would have been destroyed by the local rulers at the time of Assyria's fall. None the less, this lack of material evidence is significant for the present study in so far as it indicates that Olmstead's suggestion is (for the moment at any rate) entirely without archaeological support.

37. Hezekiah later stripped the gold from the Temple doors to pay tribute to Assyria (II Kings 18.16). For the proposed emendation see BH³; N. H. Snaith, *Kings, IB* III, 1954; Gray, *Kings, ad loc.*

38. These are included in the list of cultic apparatus removed in the course of Josiah's reformation (II Kings 23.12). *Maᶜᵃlōt 'āḥāz* in II Kings 20.9–11; Isa. 38.8 has been variously translated 'the sundial of Ahaz' and 'the steps of Ahaz', but 1QIsaᵃ has the reading *m'lwt 'lyt 'ḥz*, 'the steps of the upper chamber of Ahaz'. Cf. S. Iwry, 'The Qumran Isaiah and the End of the Dial of Ahaz', *BASOR* 147, 1957, pp. 27–33.

39. E. Schrader, *Die Keilinschriften und das Alte Testament³*, ed. H. Zimmern and H. Winckler, Berlin 1903, p. 601. Cf. more recently, A. L. Oppenheim, 'A New Prayer to the "Gods of the Night" ', AnBib 12, 1959, pp. 282–301.

40. *CML*, K I.ii.20ff.; I. iv. 2ff.; = *CTCA*, 14.73ff.; 14.165ff. In an offering list (*CTCA*, 35.50) further reference is made to sacrifice offered on a rooftop (*b.gg*), possibly to a Sun-god (cf. T. H. Gaster, 'Sun', *IDB* IV, p. 464).

41. A. S. Kapelrud, *The Ras Shamra Discoveries and the Old Testament*, ET, Oxford 1965, pp. 74–5.

42. Strabo (1st cent. BC–1st cent. AD), *Geographica* xvi.4.26; cf. W. R. Smith, *Religion of the Semites*, p. 230, n. 4.

43. Montgomery, *Kings*, p. 469; Gray, *Kings*, p. 648. See further ch. VI.

44. II Kings 16.3; II Chron. 28.2. The greatest sins of the Northern kings, according to the Deuteronomist (see especially II Kings 17.9ff.), are in following the Canaanitish bull-cults of Jeroboam (I Kings 12.25ff.) and in introducing the Phoenician gods in the time of the Omrides (I Kings 16.29ff.).

45. II Kings 16.3 (II Chron. 28.3 reads 'sons'). This practice was 'unknown to the Assyrians (except possibly at this very period through direct borrowing from Phoenicia). On the other hand, though this practice was unknown to Judah, as to Assyria, until introduced at the time of Ahaz, it is clearly attested in Phoenicia and its colonies both before and after this period. This provides a strong indication that the new cults which Ahaz introduced into Jerusalem were Phoenician rather than Assyrian' (Saggs, *op. cit.*, p. 22.)

46. II Chron. 28.2–3. See further pp. 39–41).

47. II Kings 16.4; II Chron. 28.4.

48. Josephus, *Antiquitates Judaicae*, ix. 243 (AD 93–4).

49. See further ch. III, n. 46.

50. No doubt for reasons similar to those suggested above, n. 7.

51. W. R. Smith, *op. cit.*, p. 55. Mr J. C. G. Strachan, my colleague in the Classics Department of the University of Hull, has drawn my attention to the following passage from Plato's *Laws* X 909e—910a (4th cent. BC) which expresses a very similar opinion: 'But it is the common way, especially with all women, with the sick universally, with persons in danger or any sort of distress . . . to dedicate whatever comes to hand at the moment and vow sacrifices and endowments to gods, spirits, and sons of gods, as prompted by fears of portents beheld in waking life, or by dreams.' (Translation by A. E. Taylor in E. Hamilton and H. Cairns (eds.), *The Collected Dialogues of Plato*, Bollingen Series LXXI, Pantheon Books, New York 1961, p. 1465.) There are many examples of the ways in which men have reacted to stress and fear by turning to pagan and superstitious rites, usually of a horrifying kind. For example, it was in fear and under stress that Saul consulted the witch of Endor (I Sam. 28.5ff.), that the refugees in Egypt turned to the Queen of Heaven (Jer. 44.15ff.), that Mesha of Moab sacrificed his own son (II Kings 3.26f.), and that men throughout the Western Semitic world would, like Mesha, offer their children when resistance against a besieging army seemed hopeless (cf. Ph. Derchain, 'Les plus anciens témoignages de sacrifices d'enfants chez les Sémites occidentaux', *VT* 20, 1970, pp. 351–5). There is a tradition preserved by Curtius Rufus (1st cent. AD) in his *History of Alexander* IV iii.23 that in the time of the siege of Tyre 'some even proposed renewing a sacrifice which had been discontinued for many years, and which I for my part should believe to be by no means pleasing to the gods, of offering a freeborn boy to Saturn – this sacrilege rather than sacrifice, handed down from their founders, the Carthaginians are said to have performed until the destruction of their city – and unless the elders, in accordance with whose counsel everything was done, had opposed it, the awful superstition would have prevailed over mercy.' (Translation by J. C. Rolfe, *Quintus Curtius*, Loeb Classical Library, London and Cambridge (Mass.), 1946.) Conditions were not entirely dissimilar in Ahaz's reign.

CHAPTER III

1. H. H. Rowley, *art. cit.*, *BJRL* 44, p.425.
2. Cf. Noth, *History*, p.269; Bright, *History*, p.280; Oesterley and Robinson, *History I*, p.389; Snaith, *Kings*, p.290.
3. Reading plural with LXX, Vg, Pesh and one MS of MT; see also n.5 below.
4. Gray, *Kings*, p.670.
5. J. Wellhausen, *Prolegomena to the History of Ancient Israel*, Meridian Books reprint of *Prolegomena to the History of Israel*, New York 1957, pp.46–7, 480; B. Stade, *Geschichte des Volkes Israel* I, Allgemeine Geschichte in Einzeldarstellungen, ed. W. Oncken, I.6, Berlin 1887, p.607; G. Hölscher, *Geschichte der israelitischen und jüdischen Religion*, Sammlung A. Töpelmann I.7, Leipzig 1922, pp.98–9. The use of *wāw* with the perfect in this verse in place of the expected *wāw*-consecutive may suggest the same conclusion. If *hā'ăšērā* is emended with the Versions to *hā'ăšērīm*, then *wᵉšibbar* and *wᵉkārat* may be regarded as repetitive or frequentative, but *wᵉkittat*, which describes the destruction of Nehushtan, cannot be thus explained. It may therefore be an example of simple parataxis. The editor, having written v.4*a*, then adds source material prefacing it with a simple *wāw*. *Wāw* with the perfect in narrative has been variously understood. B. Stade, 'Anmerkungen zu 2 Kö. 10–14', *ZAW* 5, 1885, pp.275–97, ref. pp.291ff., believed that it was a late phenomenon in Hebrew literature and therefore a sure sign of glossation. On this basis he excised liberally from the text of the Old Testament. Although Stade's proposals have been criticized, his influence has been lasting and may be seen in Benzinger, *Könige*, pp.192–4; Šanda, *Könige* II, pp.340–4; Kittel, *Könige*, pp. 300–3; A. F. Puukko, *Das Deuteronomium, eine literarkritische Untersuchung*, BWAT 5, Leipzig 1910, p.6; Montgomery, *Kings*, p.546; Gray, *Kings*, pp. 732ff. However, a number of commentators have found themselves unable to agree with Stade's interpretation of this construction. C. F. Burney, *Notes on the Hebrew Text of the Books of Kings*, Oxford 1903, pp.357–8, thought that it was a sign of 'decadence' in style, whilst S. R. Driver, *Hebrew Tenses*, pp.159–61, maintained that in later literature it presented 'an insoluble enigma'. E. Kautzsch (ed.) *Gesenius' Hebrew Grammar*, second English edition revised in accordance with the twenty-eighth German edition (1909) by A. E. Cowley, Oxford 1910, pp.338–9, believed that it was generally employed to express frequentative or continuous description, although he admitted that the text may sometimes be corrupt. E. König, *Historisch-comparative Syntax der hebräischen Sprache; Schlusstheil des Historisch-kritischen Lehrgebäudes des Hebräischen*, Leipzig 1897, §370n, suggested that it sometimes implied discontinuity and should be translated 'he also (did x)'. A. Jepsen, *Baumgärtel Festschrift*, p.99, suggests that it expresses simultaneity and is to be translated 'and at the same time he (did x)', but Östreicher, *op. cit*, p. 42, argues that it implies delay and carries some such meaning as 'and after some time he (did x)'. A. R. Siebens, *L'origine du code deuteronomique*, Paris 1929, pp.78–80, declared *wāw* with the perfect in narrative an error in transcription and A. Rubinstein, 'The Anomalous Perfect with *Wāw*-Conjunctive in Biblical

Hebrew', *Biblica* 44, 1963, pp.62–9, has suggested that it may result from errors in copying at a time when Aramaic influence was strong (cf. also P. Joüon, *Grammaire de l'hébreu biblique*², Scripta Pontificii Instituti Biblici, Rome, 1947, §119y–z). K. Budde, 'Das Deuteronomium und die Reform König Josias', *ZAW* 44, 1926, pp.177–244, considered that it originated in the introduction to the text of marginal notes or parallel accounts which 'raggedly began with a perfect without *wāw*. G. Bergsträsser, *Wilhelm Gesenius' Hebräische Grammatik*²⁹, Leipzig 1929, II.§9n, believed that the construction could be ancient and evidence that it was is cited by F. R. Blake, *A Resurvey of Hebrew Tenses*, Scripta Pontificii Instituti Biblici, Rome 1951, §§34, 37, and R. Meyer, 'Auffallender Erzählungsstil in einem angeblichen Auszug aus der "Chronik der Könige von Juda"', *Baumgärtel Festschrift*, pp.114–23. Finally, A. Sperber, *A Historical Grammar of Biblical Hebrew. A presentation of problems with suggestions to their solution*, Leiden 1966, pp.70–2, claims that Hebrew has no *consecutio temporum* and formulates a new rule of sequence to explain the phenomenon. In view of this vast array of often conflicting opinion, it seems likely that it will be possible to explain the construction differently in its different occurrences. For example, many of the occurrences of *wāw* with the perfect in narrative are used for description, e.g., Judg. 7.13, *wᵉnāpal*, 'and it lay fallen'. Often it is employed in a continuous or frequentative sense (instances listed by Kautzsch) and this is probably how its usage here, in II Kings 18.4a, is to be understood, as is suggested above. In many of the remaining instances suspicion is cast on the text by variant readings, e.g., *wᵉheḥᵉrīšū* in II Kings 18.36 is emended to *wayyaḥᵃrīšū* in Isa. 36.21, and *wᵉrā'ᵃtā* in II Kings 11.1 is emended in *Qᵉrē*, the Versions, many MSS and II Chron. 22.10; cf. also Judg. 16.18; I Sam. 24.11; II Sam. 19.18f.; I Kings 3.11; 12.32; 13.3; II Kings 14.7, 14; Amos 5.26. Only in a few places does it present the grammarian with 'an insoluble enigma', II Kings 18.4b being one of these (cf. also Judg. 3.23; I Sam. 17.38; II Sam. 13.18; 16.5; I Kings 21.12; II Kings 12.12; 23.4–15; Ezek. 37.2–10, where notoriously difficult, but not necessarily inexplicable, occurrences of the construction are to be found). Probably the best solution here is that proposed by Budde, that the editor has added material from an additional source in a paratactic fashion. It is also likely that this explanation will suffice for several of the instances in II Kings 23.4–15; see ch.V, n.5.

6. So R. H. Pfeiffer, *Introduction to the Old Testament*², London 1952, pp. 379–81; W. O. E. Oesterley and T. H. Robinson, *An Introduction to the Books of the Old Testament*, London 1934, pp.104–5; A. Bentzen, *Introduction to the Old Testament*⁴ II, ET, Copenhagen 1958, pp.96ff.

7. H. H. Rowley, 'Zadok and Nehushtan', *JBL* 58, 1939, pp.113–41.

8. J. Gray, 'The Canaanite God Horon', *JNES* 8, 1949, pp.27–34.

9. K. R. Joines, 'The Bronze Serpent in the Israelite Cult', *JBL* 87, 1968, pp.245–56; Gray, *Kings*, pp.670–1. Cf. also the lengthy section on the divine nature of the serpent in Philo of Byblos (1st—2nd cent. AD) as preserved in Eusebius, *Praeparatio Evangelica* (after AD 312?) I 10.45–53 (enumeration follows K. Mras [ed.], *Die Praeparatio Evangelica* I, Die griechischen christlichen Schriftsteller der ersten Jahrhunderte [*Eusebius VIII*], Berlin 1954). See also p.46 and fig.8 below.

10. A copper snake with a gilded head was found *in situ* in the Holy of Holies in the Midianite shrine at Timna in the Sinai Peninsula as the only votive offering; cf. B. Rothenberg, *Midianite Timna, Valley of the Biblical Copper Mines,* An archaeological exhibition from the excavations in the Timna Valley (Israel) 1964–1970 by the Arabah Expedition, Institute of Archaeology, Tel Aviv University, at the British Museum, October—November, 1971, London 1971, pp.19, 22; Pl.13. For discussion of Israel's relations with the family of Jethro, see H. H. Rowley, *From Joseph to Joshua. Biblical Traditions in the Light of Archaeology,* Schweich Lectures 1948, London 1950, pp.149ff.

11. First speech: II Kings 18.19–25 and Isa. 36.4–10.
　　Second speech: II Kings 18.28–35 and Isa. 36.13–20.
References in the text are to II Kings 18.

12. See p.60.

13. This seems to be the basis for the fear he expresses before Yahweh, the dominant theme in II Kings 19.

14. Östreicher, *op. cit.,* pp.49–50, and M. Weinfeld, 'Cult Centralization in Israel in the Light of a Neo-Babylonian Analogy', *JNES* 23, 1964, pp.202–12, both argue that Judaean attempts to centralize the cult may be compared with Nabonidus bringing the gods of his kingdom into Babylon, the purpose being to prevent the enemy from gaining control over the god(s) of the land and to concentrate the power of the god(s) in the oppressed city. But see further below, n.41.

15. *ANET,* pp.287–8.

16. Nehushtan itself was perhaps neither trivial nor unknown in ancient Judah (see p.19 and nn.7–10 above), but it would certainly have been so in comparison with Assyrian gods, if they had been officially present in the Temple.

17. See further, pp.17–19.

18. B. S. Childs, *Isaiah and the Assyrian Crisis,* SBT, second series 3, 1967, p.107.

19. Since the descriptions of the Passover (II Chron. 30) and the ritual reparations (II Chron. 29) are concerned with purely internal Yahwistic reform, they are not relevant to the present discussion.

20. E. L. Curtis and A. A. Madsen, *A Critical and Exegetical Commentary on the Books of Chronicles,* ICC, 1910, p.463. They consider that these chapters (II Chron. 29ff.) are of little value as a source of information for the history of Hezekiah's reign (p.462).

21. J. Morgenstern, 'The Gates of Righteousness', *HUCA* 6, 1929, pp.1–37; cf. II Chron. 29.3 gives the date here as the first of Tishri.

22. To my knowledge no one has used this argument to support the thesis that Hezekiah was purging the Temple of Assyrian gods imported by Ahaz. J. Morgenstern, *art. cit.,* does maintain on similar grounds that the Chronicler's information supports the view that Ahaz had introduced solar elements to the Temple cultus, but he argues that these elements were Phoenician rather than Assyrian in origin. Cf. *idem, The Fire upon the Altar,* pp.102–13.

23. *Mishnah Sukkah* 5.4: 'Our fathers when they were in this place turned

with their backs toward the Temple of the Lord and their faces toward the east, and they worshipped the sun toward the east; but as for us, our eyes are turned toward the Lord.' (Translation by H. Danby, *The Mishnah translated from the Hebrew with introduction and brief explanatory notes.* Oxford 1933, p. 180). Although this is a direct reference to Ezek.8.16, it is likely that its inclusion in the Mishnah indicates continuing opposition to similar practices in post-exilic times.

24. See p. 48.

25. J. Morgenstern, *op. cit.*, pp.102–13, and *art. cit.* But on the value of the views expressed in Morgenstern's book, see the comments by S. H. Hooke, *A Decade of Bible Bibliography. The Book Lists of the Society for Old Testament Study 1957–1966*, ed. G. W. Anderson, Oxford 1967, p. 530.

26. See p. 52.

27. Östreicher, *op. cit.*, pp.53–5, maintained that the solar cults in Jerusalem in the Assyrian period were dedicated to the worship of Shamash-Ashur (cf. also recently W. Eichrodt, *Ezekiel, a commentary*, ET, OTL, 1970, p.125). But Gressmann, *ZAW* 42, p.323, points out that Shamash = Ashur was not an Assyrian equation. G. van Driel, *The Cult of Aššur*, Assen 1969, has nothing to say of such an equation and K. Tallqvist, *Der assyrische Gott*, SO IV.3, 1932, pp.4 off., 106ff., maintains that the evidence is not strong enough to support a definition of Ashur as a Sun-god. See also E. Dhorme, *Religions*, pp.162–4. That Ashur assimilated the attributes of other gods, see *GMVO*, p.44.

28. That the mention of centralization (II Kings 18.22; Isa. 36.7) probably belongs to the original, historical core of the Rabshakeh's first speech, see B. S. Childs, *op. cit.*, pp.82–5.

29. II Kings 18.16. See ch.II, n.37.

30. Y. Aharoni, 'Arad: its Inscriptions and Temple', *BA* 31, 1968, pp. 1–32.

31. As maintained by E. W. Todd, 'The Reforms of Hezekiah and Josiah', *SJT* 9, 1956, pp.288–93.

32. It is generally recognized that the Chronicler was particularly concerned with the unity of 'all Israel', probably because of the Samaritan problem of his own day (cf. A. C. Welch, *The Work of the Chronicler, its purpose and its date*, Schweich Lectures 1938, London 1939, pp.108–10; W. A. L. Elmslie, *The First and Second Books of Chronicles*, IB III, 1954, pp.344–5; F. L. Moriarty, 'The Chronicler's Account of Hezekiah's Reform', *CBQ* 27, 1965, pp.399–406, ref. p.403), and it may be for this reason that Hezekiah is said to have postponed the celebration for one month so that the Northerners could purify themselves. (Contrast S. Talmon, 'Divergences in Calendar-Reckoning in Ephraim and Judah', *VT* 8, 1958, pp.48–74, who argues that Hezekiah was adapting the date of Passover to suit the calendar used in the North.) This conclusion, however, must be balanced by the consideration that the Chronicler is also intent on preserving purity and exclusiveness in the community (cf. P. R. Ackroyd, *The Age of the Chronicler*, The Selwyn Lectures 1970, Supplement to *Colloquium* – the Australian and New Zealand Theological Review, Auckland 1970, pp.38, 55f). It has also been argued recently that the concern of the Chronicler was not so much with a Samaritan schism as 'with the maintenance of the unity of Judaism under the hegemony of Jerusalem'

(R. J. Coggins, 'The Old Testament and Samaritan Origins', *ASTI* 6, 1967–8, pp. 35–48, ref. p. 46).

33. Whilst arguments for the historicity of the Chronicler's account have been put forward (e.g. Welch, *op. cit.*, pp. 97–121; Talmon, *art. cit.*), the conclusion which seems most apt is that held by J. B. Segal, *The Hebrew Passover from Earliest Times to A.D. 70*, London Oriental Series 12, London 1963, pp. 18–19, who argues that II Chron. 30 represents a later attempt to outdo Josiah's Passover by the introduction of the more correct liturgical practices of a later age.

34. As maintained, for example, by Nicholson, *Deuteronomy and Tradition*, pp. 98–9.

35. So Oesterley and Robinson, *History* I, p. 380.

36. H. H. Rowley, 'The Prophet Jeremiah and the Book of Deuteronomy', *Studies in Old Testament Prophecy presented to Professor T. H. Robinson*, ed. H. H. Rowley, Edinburgh 1950, pp. 157–74, ref. p. 164 (now in his *From Moses to Qumran: (Studies in the Old Testament*, London 1963, pp. 187–208).

37. For bibliography, see Nicholson, *op. cit.*, p. 58, n. 1. For recent expression of a completely contrasting point of view, see G. J. Wenham, 'Deuteronomy and the Central Sanctuary', *Tyndale Bulletin*, 1971, pp. 103–18.

38. On the identification of the *'am-hā'āreṣ* see the discussion and bibliography in E. W. Nicholson, 'The Meaning of the Expression עַם הָאָרֶץ in the Old Testament', *JSS* 10, 1965, pp. 59–66.

39. Cf. the fact that Jeremiah was banned from the Temple and Amos was turned away from Bethel because their message was unacceptable (Jer. 36.5; Amos 7.13).

40. This date is disputed. 727 and 720 BC have also been suggested; see commentaries, *ad loc.*

41. Several theories about the background to the demand for centralization have been proposed. For example, it has been suggested that its roots lie in the amphictyonic ideal of a central sanctuary; cf. von Rad, *Deuteronomy*, p. 90; M. Noth, 'The Laws in the Pentateuch: their Assumptions and Meaning', *The Laws in the Pentateuch and Other Essays*, Edinburgh and London 1966, pp. 1–107, ref. pp. 28–36; G. E. Wright, *Deuteronomy*, IB II, 1953, p. 324; Nicholson, *op. cit.*, p. 69. Others have maintained that centralization of the cult is the logical outcome of David's political centralization in the city of Jerusalem; cf. A. Bentzen, *Die josianische Reform und ihre Voraussetzungen*, Copenhagen 1926, pp. 68–72; J. Pedersen, *Israel: its life and culture* III–IV, Copenhagen 1940, pp. 578ff.; E. Robertson, 'Temple and Torah', *The Old Testament Problem: a reinvestigation*, University of Manchester Publications 307, Manchester 1950, pp. 33–55. It has also been argued that the miraculous deliverance of Jerusalem in 701 BC added considerable impetus to the centralizing tendency; cf. V. Maag, 'Erwägungen zur deuteronomischen Kultzentralisation', *VT* 6, 1956, pp. 10–18. Again, it has been suggested that Hezekiah first centralized as an act of political necessity; cf. E. W. Nicholson, 'The Centralization of the Cult in Deuteronomy', *VT* 13, 1963, pp. 380–9; Weinfeld, *art. cit.*, and Östreicher, *op. cit.* (see n. 14 above). Some scholars believe that centralization depends mainly on a prior demand for cultic purity; cf. Siebens, *L'origine du code deuteronomique*, pp. 97–118. Thus Östreicher,

op. cit., and A. C. Welch, *The Code of Deuteronomy: a new theory of its origin*, London 1924, argue that Deuteronomy's demand for cultic unity is secondary to its demand for cultic purity. But there have also been those, particularly amongst older scholars, who have felt that the main influence on Judah's reformers was the demand of Deuteronomism; cf. E. Sellin, *Introduction to the Old Testament*, ET of the third German edition, London 1923, pp.73ff.; G. A. Smith, *The Book of Deuteronomy*, CBSC, 1918, p.cii; C. Steuernagel, *Das Deuteronomium*, HKAT I.3.1, 1923, p.xiv; E. König, *Das Deuteronomium*, KAT 3, Leipzig 1917, pp.48ff.; and more recently H. Junker, 'Die Entstehungszeit des Ps.78 und das Deuteronomium', *Biblica* 34, 1953, pp.487–500.

42. II Kings 18.13ff. Noth and a number of other scholars identify Hezekiah's rebellion with his reformation and thus date the two at the same time.

43. Noth, *History*, p.269. Bright, *History*, p.286, avoids the difficulty thus: 'That Sennacherib did not return to take vengeance is best explained by the fact that Hezekiah died the following year (687/6). His son Manasseh gave up the rebellion . . .'

44. E.g., Isa.30.1–7; 31.1–3.

45. II Kings 19.35–6; II Chron. 32.20–2. On the historicity of this record, see Childs, *op. cit.*, pp. 101–3.

46. Whilst the presence of Assyrian gods may be supposed, the historian's failure to mention them must be regarded as a serious indication that they had no official status. It is also significant that the picture of paganism painted by the eighth-century prophets is in accord with the general conclusions set forth above. In Israel before 722 BC the cults of the *bāmōt* flourished with their *'ašērim* and *maṣṣēbōt* (Hos. 10.1–2) and with their fertility orgies (Hos. 4.11–13), as did other fertility rites and cultic prostitution (Hos. 2.15, EVV 2.13; 4.9–14; 9.1–2). These and the worship of Baal (Hos. 2.18–19, EVV 2.16–17; 11.2; 13.1–2) belong to the indigenous cults of Canaan, as did the Bull-cult of Jeroboam (Hos. 8.5; 10.5, 8; 13.1–2) and other unspecified idolatry (Hos. 13.1–2; 14.9, EVV 14.8), but there is no suggestion in the prophetic writings that any kind of cult that could have been Assyrian existed in Israel between the years 734 and 722 BC. As in Israel, general idolatry (Isa. 2.8, 20; 10.10) and the cults of the *bāmōt* with their *'ašērim* and *maṣṣēbōt* (Isa. 27.9; Micah 5.9–14, EVV 5.10–15) flourished in eighth-century Judah. Adonis gardens may have been planted (Isa. 17.10–11; cf. W. F. Albright, 'Islam and the Religions of the Ancient Orient', *JAOS* 60, 1940, pp.283–301, ref. pp.297–8). Sorcerers and soothsayers (Micah 5.9–14) and soothsayers like the Philistines (Isa. 2.6) were found in the land. Only once is a possible Assyrian presence suggested. Isa. 2.6 also mentions an abundance of men from the east (if the MT reading *ki māle'ū miqqedem* is correct), or men who imitated eastern practices (if the reading *ke'imiqqedem* suggested by LXX, Vg and Pesh is more acceptable), but the context implies that they were no more the representatives of official cults than were their Philistine counterparts. If they were from Mesopotamia, their presence is expected in this age of international upheaval when Assyrian armies dominated the west. However, in the Old Testament Assyria and Babylonia are generally located in the north, not the east; cf. Jer. 3.12, 18; 16.15; 23.8; 31.8; 46.10; Ezek. 26.7; Zeph. 2.13; Zech. 2.6–7; see R. A. Bowman, 'The North Country', *IDB* III, p.560. By contrast, the peoples of

the east were the inhabitants of the Syrian desert and Arabia, possibly including the Transjordanian peoples in Edom and Moab (Isa. 11.14); see
D. S. Margoliouth, 'Children of the East', *HDB* I, p.635. In Gen. 29.1 the
east is regarded as the home of Laban, but it may be that the term is here used
in a very broad and general manner; see S. Cohen, 'The People of the East',
IDB II, p.4; G. von Rad, *Genesis, a commentary*[2], ET, OTL, 1963, p.283;
S. R. Driver, *The Book of Genesis*, WC, 1904, p.268. It would therefore appear
that Isa. 2.6 suggests the infiltration of Arabian or other Transjordanian
paganism or culture into Judah, rather than an official presence of Assyrian
religion.

CHAPTER IV

1. See A. Jepsen, *Die Quellen des Königsbuches*, Halle 1953, p.25. On the
problem of the editing of Kings, see Gray, *Kings*, pp.6ff., and works cited
there.

2. Gray, *Kings*, p.705. See also Ackroyd, *The Age of the Chronicler*, p.45,
who believes that in the Deuteronomist's history of the reigns of Ahaz to
Josiah the 'alternating pattern of good and bad kings oversimplifies the
account'. He suggests that this pattern is theological rather than historical,
particularly in its portrayal of Manasseh as the king ultimately responsible for
the downfall of Judah.

3. See pp.47ff.

4. See p.8 and ch.VI, n.115.

5. II Kings 21.2; II Chron. 33.2.

6. II Kings 21.3; II Chron. 33.3. The history of the *bāmōt* is in many respects
obscure, but there is plenty of evidence in the Old Testament to suggest that
they were places where the Canaanite fertility cults flourished, particularly in
late pre-exilic times. The Israelites seem to have regarded them as legitimate
Yahweh shrines from earliest times (I Sam. 9.12–25; 10.5, 13; I Kings 3.2–4),
and even in the days of Hezekiah and Josiah (II Kings 18.22; II Chron. 32.12;
Isa. 36.7; II Kings 23.9; II Chron. 33.17). However, Ezekiel is of the opinion
that the religion of the Judaean Levites was not pure Yahwism (44.9–14) and
his criticisms probably result from the infiltration of Canaanite fertility rituals
into the *bāmōt* cults in later monarchic times. Thus we find the Northern
bāmōt associated with the bull-cults of Jeroboam (I Kings 12.31–2; 13.32–3;
II Chron. 11.15; Hos. 10.8) and with Canaanite practices (II Kings 17.9–11),
whilst the *bāmōt* of Judah are marked by the presence of *'ašērîm* and *maṣṣēbōt*
(I Kings 14.23; II Chron. 14.3, 5; 17.6; 31.1; 33.19; 34.3; Jer. 17.2–3) and
the worship of Baal (II Kings 21.3; II Chron. 33.3; 34.4). These Southern
shrines were often sited 'on every high hill and under every green tree' and
were frequently condemned as places where fertility rites of a sexual nature
were performed (II Kings 16.4; II Chron. 28.4; Jer. 2.20; 3.6, 13, 21ff.;
13.27; 17.2–3; Ezek. 16.16; 20.28–9; cf. Hos. 4.11–13, 17–19; see also n.59
below and ch.III, n.46). There can therefore be little doubt that by the time
of Manasseh fertility rituals were a marked feature of the *bāmōt* cults. See
further de Vaux, *Ancient Israel*, pp.284–6.

7. As II Chron. 33.6 suggests. The sacrifice of his son can hardly have been in imitation of an Assyrian practice; see ch. II, n.45. On the Molech cult, see pp. 39ff.

8. So Albright, *op. cit.*, p.164. It is not clear from II Kings 21.3 how far Manasseh's abuses corresponded to Ahab's. I Kings 16.31ff. suggests that Ahab instituted an official, central cult of Baal and Asherah in Samaria, but the apostasy under Manasseh may have been more local and popular. Certainly the Chronicler seems to think of a revival of the local *beˤālīm* and *ʾašērōt* cults of the *bāmōt*, but Chronicles generally prefers the plural to the singular forms. From eleven occurrences Chronicles uses the singular, *ʾašērā*, only once (II Chron. 15.16, and here the plural form would be impossible), whereas Kings uses the singular on twelve out of sixteen occasions (see the Concordances). The feminine plural, *ʾašērōt*, is unusual (cf. also II Chron. 19.3), *ʾašērīm* being the more common form. Thus it would seem that the Chronicler's rewriting has obscured the correspondence with Ahab's apostasy at this point. But the problem is not so easily solved, for LXX, Vg and Pesh of II Kings 21.3 also make the Asherah plural, although they retain the singular for Baal. Nevertheless, II Kings 21.7 leaves little doubt that the cult of the mother-goddess did occupy a prominent place in the Temple under Manasseh.

9. J. Scharbert, *Die Propheten Israels um 600 v. Chr.*, Cologne 1967, pp. 12–13, argues that the Canaanite Asherah is never in the Old Testament said to have been represented by a carved image.

10. Deut. 16.21 prohibits the planting of an Asherah-tree beside the altar of Yahweh. This is slightly different from the erection of an idol, but see more fully the discussion on pp. 21–3.

11. See ch. III, n.46.

12. I Kings 5.15–20 (EVV 5.1–6) relates how Solomon made an agreement with Hiram for the supply of materials for the building of the Temple. We also read that Solomon made extensive use of Phoenician labour (5.18, EVV) and engaged a Tyrian master-craftsman for the construction of the Temple ornaments and its cultic apparatus (7.13–47). The result was that the finished building probably corresponded closely in structure and decoration with the temples of the Phoenician cities; see A. Parrot, *The Temple*, pp. 15–55. On the foreign cults introduced as a result of Solomon's marriages, see I Kings 11.1–5 and II Kings 23.13.

13. II Kings 8.18, 26–7; II Kings 11; see ch. II, n.13.

14. R. Patai, 'The Goddess Asherah', *JNES* 24, 1965. pp. 37–52. He fails to distinguish clearly between the cult of the Asherah image in Samaria and the local *ʾašērīm* cults of the *bāmōt*, but his study none the less presents a useful collection of the evidence. On the history of the Phoenician Asherah, see Comte du Mesnil du Buisson, 'Origine et évolution du panthéon de Tyr', *RHR* 164, 1963, pp. 133–63.

15. The note in II Kings 18.4 probably relates the removal of *ʾašērīm* on local *bāmōt* rather than the abolition of an Asherah image from the Temple (see ch. III, n.3). II Chron. 24.18 claims that Joash patronized these local cults in the later years of his reign. Cf. Isa. 17.8; 27.9; Micah 5.12–13 (EVV 13–14) which also suggest the existence of these local *ʾašērīm* cults in the time of Ahaz and Hezekiah.

16. For example, it is not unlikely that Athaliah's cult was dedicated to the veneration of Asherah as well as of Baal (II Kings 11).

17. And hence Scharbert's conclusion (*loc. cit.*) that the goddess in question cannot have been the Canaanite Asherah, but must be the Assyrian Ishtar.

18. Cf. II Chron. 33.19; 34.3, 4, 7; Deut. 7.5; 12.3. The only other word used in the Old Testament to describe the image made for Asherah is the apparently derogatory term, *mipleṣet*, in I Kings 15.13.

19. The Versions disagree about the meaning of the word *semel*, but all (except Pesh) accept the reading *hā'ᵃšērā* in II Kings 21.7.

20. H. Torczyner, 'Semel Ha-qin'ah Ha-maqneh', *JBL* 65, 1946, pp. 293–302, dismisses the derivation from the Accadian *lamassu* with the meaning 'bull-god' (not one of the meanings given in *AHw*, pp. 532–3) on the grounds that the *semel* in Phoenician is never theriomorphic, but his suggested derivation from the Accadian *šamallû* (a commercial agent) is rather far-fetched and is rejected by Rudolph, *Chronikbücher*, p. 314 (see further below, n. 25).

21. Allbright, *op. cit.*, pp. 165–6 and 221, n. 121. His suggestion is accepted by W. Zimmerli, *Ezechiel* I, BKAT 12, Neukirchen-Vluyn, 1969, p. 214.

22. *KAI* 26 C IV 13ff. (Kartepe, 720 BC) refers to the idol (not extant) accompanying the inscription as a 'divine image', *sml (h)'lm*; *KAI* 41 (Tamassos, 363 BC) records the erection of a *sml* to Reshef-Eleios, Apollo of Helos; *KAI* 33 (Kition, 325 BC) dedicates a *smlt* to Lady Ashtart.

23. The plural, *smlm*, is used of funerary images in *KAI* 40.3 (Idalion, 255 BC), and *KAI* 43.2 (Lapethos, 275 BC) reads 'This *sml* is that of myself, Jathon-ba'al . . .', but both of these inscriptions suggest connection with a god. The former invokes the blessing of Reshef-MKL and the latter was erected in the temple of Melqart.

24 As was the image referred to in *KAI* 33.2: [*s*]*mlt* '[*z*] . . . *mnḥšt*. The feminine form, *smlt*, is clearly used in agreement with the gender of the deity (cf. the same form in *CIS* I.40), but no conclusion about the nature of the *semel* in II Chron. 33.7 can depend on this observation, since there is no means of determining whether Hebrew ever knew a feminine form of the noun.

25. H. Bar-Deroma, 'Kadesh-Barnea', *PEQ* 1964, pp. 101–34, ref. p. 132, believes that the phrase *mōšab sēmel haqqin'ā hammaqneh* in Ezek. 8.3 defines the *semel* as some kind of mother-goddess tree-symbol, on the grounds that *maqneh* is a secondary form of *qāneh*, meaning 'reed' or 'cane'. But it seems equally if not more correct to maintain that *maqneh* is the *Hip'îl* participle of the verb *qānā*. Torczyner, *art. cit.*, suggests that the roots *qānā* (to buy) and *qānā'* (to be jealous) are often confused and that *haqqin'ā* should be related to the former in the present verse. *Maqneh* should now, he argues, be pointed *miqneh*, a noun which denotes cattle, oxen or sheep. Basing his argument on a comparison with the Accadian *šamallû*, a commercial agent who buys and sells for a master, or even redeems prisoners of war for his own king, he defines the *semel* as Asherah seated on a throne in the capacity of a redeeming agent receiving the sacrifices of cattle, oxen or sheep. Rudolph, *Chronik-bücher*, p. 314, rightly objects to this rather far-fetched conclusion on the grounds that the meaning 'statue', which *semel* has in the Phoenician inscriptions, can hardly be derived from 'commercial agent'. Eichrodt, *Ezekiel*,

p. 122, favours a suggestion made by Herrmann that the *semel* was an image, not of wrathful jealousy but of passionate love; cf. NEB: 'image of Lust (to rouse lustful passion)'. It may therefore have been an anthropomorphic idol of the mother-goddess with emphasized sexual features.

Eichrodt also argues that Ezekiel's *semel* must be identified with the Asherah *semel* set in the Temple in Manasseh's time and probably restored after the death of Josiah. Zimmerli, *op. cit.*, pp. 214–5, expresses doubt about such an equation on the grounds that Manasseh's image was in the Temple, whereas Ezekiel's image was at the entrance to the Temple court. He therefore favours Albright's suggestion that the *semel* was a slab-image set in a niche in the wall. There has, however, been some debate about the precise meaning of the word *mōšab* in this text. Albright's suggestion that it was a niche depends partly on the use of the word *mtb* in *CML*, SS i. 19 (= *CTCA*, 23.19): *mtbt.ʾelm.tmn*, 'the niches of the gods are eight'. But T. H. Gaster, 'Ezekiel and the Mysteries', *JBL* 60; 1941, pp. 289–310, ref. p. 309, appeals to the same passage to support his translation 'throne'. Bar-Deroma, *art. cit.*, suggests the translation 'pedestal' on the grounds that his tree-image could not have sat on a throne, but Torczyner earlier pointed out that *mōšāb* is never used to designate the pedestal of an idol and must be translated 'seat' or 'throne'.

26. *KAI* 26 C IV. 13ff.

27. Cf. Deut. 4.16; II Chron. 33.7. The term *semel* may even have been imported with Manasseh's idol. Deut. 4.16 possibly provides the earliest example of the word in the Old Testament. A. C. Welch, *Deuteronomy: the framework to the code*, London 1932, pp. 30–1, described the passage in which this verse occurs as a Deuteronomic 'fragment' and most scholars would agree that it was not in *Urdeuteronomium*, but it could, none the less, be a fairly old unit of Deuteronomic tradition. Ezekiel's vision in ch. 8 is dated in the sixth year after the fall of Jerusalem in 597 BC, but the paganism in the Temple which the chapter describes had doubtless been a feature of Jerusalemite apostasy for some years before that date and may have first appeared at any time during the reign of Jehoiakim when Josiah's purges had lost their effect. It is also possible that these cults represent, in part at least, a revival of the paganism in the Temple before Josiah's reformation. The objection to equating Ezekiel's *semel* with that mentioned in II Chron. 33, on the grounds that one was situated beside the gate of the court and the other was in the Temple itself (see above, n. 25), need not be conclusive. If the cult of this particular goddess was revived after the death of Josiah, it need not necessarily have had its cult image on exactly the same spot in the Temple precincts. C. C. Torrey, *Pseudo-Ezekiel and the Original Prophecy*, Yale Oriental Series. Researches 18, New Haven 1930, pp. 64ff., based his argument that the book of Ezekiel was a pseudepigraph purporting to come from the reign of Manasseh largely on the similarities to be seen between the descriptions of apostasy in Ezekiel and II Kings 21. These similarities are perhaps best explained by positing, as most scholars do, a resurgence of Manasseh's cults during the reign of Jehoiakim; see, for example, Eichrodt, *Ezekiel*, p. 122; J. B. Taylor, *Ezekiel, an introduction and commentary*, Tyndale Old Testament Commentaries, London 1969, p. 98.

28. If the *semel* was dedicated to Astarte, then the cult of the goddess may have been in some way connected with the worship of the stars which flourished at this time. On the astral aspect of the Phoenician Astarte, see p. 51. Astarte (Ashtoreth) of the Sidonians was already revered in the precincts of Jerusalem (I Kings 11.5; II Kings 23.13). It has been suggested that with the passage of time the two goddesses, Asherah and Astarte, became fused and identified amongst the Canaanites (Kapelrud, *op. cit.*, p.62), but there appears to be little evidence to support this conclusion. The two goddesses did have certain features in common (J. W. McKay, 'Helel and the Dawn-Goddess: a re-examination of the myth in Isaiah XIV 12–15', *VT* 20, 1970, pp.451–64, ref. p.462) and it is possible that a degree of confusion existed. See also below pp.45ff., 51.

29. I Kings 10.1–10. But on the location of Sheba, see J. A. Montgomery, *Arabia and the Bible*, The Library of Biblical Studies, ed. H. M. Orlinsky, New York 1969 (reprint; first published in 1934), p.61, n.11; Gray, *Kings*, pp. 258–60.

30. G. W. van Beek and A. Jamme, 'An Inscribed South Arabian Clay Stamp from Bethel', *BASOR* 151, 1958, pp.9–16. The discovery of this seal may suggest that the shrine at Bethel bought its incense from South Arabian traders (see also Gray, *loc. cit.*), but there has been some debate about the value of this find as archaeological evidence for the history of Bethel's relations with South Arabia. See A. Jamme and G. W. van Beek, 'The South-Arabian Clay Stamp from Bethel Again', *BASOR* 163, 1961, pp.15–18; Y. Yadin, 'An Inscribed South-Arabian Clay Stamp from Bethel?', *BASOR* 196, 1969, pp.37–45; G. W. van Beek and A. Jamme, 'The Authenticity of the Bethel Stamp Seal', *BASOR* 199, 1970, pp.59–65; J. L. Kelso, 'A Reply to Yadin's Article on the Finding of the Bethel Seal', *BASOR* 199, 1970, p.65.

31. See also ch.III, n.46 for the possibility of Arabian influence in Judah before the time of Manasseh.

32. *ANET*, p.286; see also H. Tadmor, 'The Campaigns of Sargon II of Assur: a Chronological-Historical Study', *JCS* 12, 1958, pp.77–100. It may also be that Hezekiah employed Arab mercenaries at the time of Sennacherib's invasion in 701 BC; cf. Montgomery, *Arabia and the Bible*, pp.61–2.

33. *ANET*, pp.284, 285, 291–2.

34. II Kings 20.12ff.

35. II Chron. 33.1 = II Kings 21.1; II Chron. 33.21 = II Kings 21.19.

36. Cf. I Kings 15.10.

37. I Kings 15.2. Of course, there is here the possibility of a scribal error and it may be that the mothers of Abijah and Asa did not have the same name originally and were not the same person, as some commentators have suggested.

38. Presumably the names of the mothers of the remaining kings of Judah, Jehoahaz, Jehoiakim, Jehoiachin and Zedekiah, were omitted from the Chronicler's history automatically, following the precedent set in modifying the introductions to the reigns of Manasseh, Amon and Josiah.

39. Num. 33.33; Deut. 10.7.

40. Montgomery, *Kings*, pp.521–2; Gray, *Kings*, p.711. So *contra* Bright, *History*, p.281, who locates Jotbah in the Galilean area.

41. Montgomery, Gray, *loc. cit.*

42. The root *šlm* was also widely used in Israel in the formation of personal names, particularly after the seventh century BC; e.g. *šelōmīt* (cf. I Chron. 3.19), *šelōmōt* (cf. I Chron. 24.22). At an earlier time the root was used by David in naming his sons *'abšālōm* and *šelōmōh*; Maacah's father was called *'abīšālōm*; one of the last kings of Israel bore the name *šallūm* (cf. also Josiah's son, Jer. 22.11, and various other persons in this period, II Kings 22.14; Jer. 32.7; 35.4). From the Arabian inscriptions there are numerous examples of names formed from the root *šlm*; e.g. *šlmt*, daughter of *yrḫy*, appears on a sepulchral inscription from *Qaṣr el-Ḥayeh* (*CIS* II.3, no. 4234), and *šlmw* was the name of the sister of a Nabataean king (*CIS* II.1, no. 210). Cf. also *šlmn* (*CIS* II.1, nos. 294, 302), *šlmw* (*CIS* II.1, nos. 320A, 363, 440); *šlmy*, *šlmt*, *šlm'lt* are also frequently recurring forms. The Hebrew form *mešullemet*, however, is found only once in ancient writing (II Kings 21.19 apart), namely at Elephantine in the fifth century BC (A. Vincent, *op. cit.*, p.407), but the masculine form *mešullām* appears in II Kings 22.3. (It may also be argued, however, that this Meshullam was of Arabian descent. He gave his son the name *'aṣalyāhū*, the first component of which M. Noth, *Die israelitischen Personennamen im Rahmen der gemeinsemitischen Namengebung*, BWANT III.10, Stuttgart, 1929, p.193, relates to the Arabic verb *'aṣula*, 'to be distinguished'.) Thus, although the root is fairly common in Hebrew names, considering Meshullemeth's parentage and place of origin, and considering the popularity of the root *šlm* in the formation of Arabian names, it is not at all unlikely that her name signifies Arabian parentage. The transformation of an original Arabian *šlmt* to the Hebrew *mešullemet* by adding *mēm*-preformative and reduplicating the *lāmed* can be paralleled in Biblical Hebrew; cf. *bānī* (II Sam. 23.36) becomes *mebunnay* (II Sam. 23.27) by the same process. (The Hebrew in II Sam. 23.27, 36 is, however, possibly corrupt; cf. BH³.) Although the root *šlm* is also found in Phoenician personal names, it always appears as a component part of the name only, e.g. *yknšlm* (*CIS* I.1, no. 10).

43. S. Yeivin, 'The Sepulchres of the Kings of the House of David', *JNES* 7, 1948, pp.30–45, believes that the Chronicler has often preserved more accurate details about royal burials than those offered by the Deuteronomist, but he does not try to explain why the Chronicler chose to omit the reference to the Garden of Uzza at this point, although he accepts the information in Kings as historically correct.

44. *began-'uzzā'*. Compare II Kings 21.18 with II Chron. 33.20 and II Kings 21.25–6 with II Chron. 33.24–5.

45. Cf. Stade, *Geschichte* I, p.569.

46. Cf. O. C. Whitehouse, 'Uzziah', *HDB* IV, pp.843–4; Yeivin, *art. cit.*, p.35.

47. Whitehouse, *loc. cit.*; Gray, *Kings*, pp. 710–1. *Al-'Uzzā* is Venus as the morning star (*GMVO*, pp.476, 548).

48. Solomon's foreign marriages resulted in the introduction of several pagan cults to the precincts of Jerusalem (I Kings 11.1–8); Rehoboam's wife, Maacah, daughter of Abishalom, whose name is certainly not Yahwistic, erected an image to Asherah in the city (I Kings 15.10–13); Ahab's marriage to Jezebel brought the Sidonian Baal and Asherah to Samaria (I Kings

16.31-3); and in consequence of Jehoram's marriage to Ahab's daughter, Athaliah, a temple for the Sidonian Baal was erected in Jerusalem (II Kings 8.18; 11.1ff.).

49. *ANET*, p.291.

50. *ANET*, p.294.

51. E.g., Rudolph, *Chronikbücher*, p.317; Bright, *History*, pp.310-13; Myers, *Chronicles* II, pp.197-9. It is not at all clear why the Chronicler thought that Manasseh was taken to Babylon rather than to Nineveh. P. R. Ackroyd has suggested to me the possibility that the Chronicler has deliberately written 'Babylon' rather than the name of an Assyrian centre to emphasize that Manasseh's captivity and repentance is a 'type' of the subsequent captivity and restoration of Judah. Sellin, *Geschichte* I, p.280f. (cf. Rudolph, *loc. cit.*) claims that the Assyrian king frequently resided in Babylon after the crushing of the Babylonian revolt, but he cites no source for his information.

52. That is, if '*Osnappar* in Ezra 4.10, who is said to have settled various nations in Samaria and the rest of the province Beyond the River, may be identified with Ashurbanipal.

53. For a completely different interpretation of Manasseh's visit to Babylon, see ch. VII, n.32.

54. Cf. Rudolph, *Chronikbücher*, p. 317.

55. A. Malamat, 'The Historical Background to the Assassination of Amon, King of Judah', *IEJ* 3, 1953, pp.26-9.

56. N. M. Nicolsky, 'Pascha im Kulte des jerusalemischen Tempels', *ZAW* 45, 1927, pp.171-90, ref. p.184.

57. That is, if any weight is to be given to the consideration that his son's name, Amon, may be Egyptian.

58. See pp.49ff.

59. The picture of apostasy in seventh-century Judah, as portrayed by Jeremiah and Zephaniah, is essentially the same as that painted by the earlier prophets (see ch. III, n.46). Idolatry (Jer. 1.16; 25.6), the worship of Baal (Zeph. 1.4; Jer. 2.8, 23; 7.9; 9.13, EVV 14; 11.12-13, 17; 23.27; 32.29, 35), augury (Jer. 10.2), the cults of the *bāmōt* (Jer. 2.20; 3.13, 21ff.; 13.27; 17.2; 32.35) with their *'ăšērīm* and *maṣṣēbōt* (Jer. 2.27; 3.9; 17.2) and cultic prostitution (Jer. 2.20, 33; 3.1ff., 6, 9, 13; 5.7; 13.27) all continued in the land. In addition, altars had been erected in the streets of Jerusalem (Jer. 11.12-13; 44.21), the Molech cult flourished in the Hinnom Valley (Jer. 2.23; 7.30ff.; 19.4ff.; 32.35), the authority of the Ammonite Milkom was recognized (Zeph. 1.5) and the Host of Heaven was revered (Zeph. 1.2-9; Jer. 8.2; 19.13). Apart from the worship of the Host of Heaven and the Queen of Heaven (Jer. 7.18; 44.17-19), all the cults mentioned by the prophets were indigenous. Even the astral cults may have been partly indigenous (see ch. VI below) and they hardly represented official Assyrian religion, for their devotees worshipped on the roofs of houses (Jer. 19.13; Zeph. 1.5) and in the streets of the city (Jer. 7.17; 44.17), the implication being that these cults were local and popular, not national. Frequent reference is also made in the book of Jeremiah and in the writings of the Deuteronomist to 'other gods' ('*ĕlōhīm* '*ăḥērīm*) and it is natural to suspect that such a general expression, although not limited to the era of Assyrian supremacy (cf. Ex. 20.3; 23.13; 34.14;

Hos. 3.1; some of these may be Deuteronomic), might cloak allusions to Assyrian deities. Unfortunately this is nevei evident. In the Deuteronomic writings the expression often explicitly refers to Canaanite gods (Deut. 6.14; Judg. 2.12, 17, 19; 10.13) and, when it does obviously refer to Mesopotamian gods, it also refers to the patriarchal period (Josh. 24.2, 16) or to the Exile (Jer. 16.13). '*elōhē* (*han*)*nēkar* and ('*elōhīm*) *zārīm* are also common expressions in the writing of this period, although again not limited to it, but once more they may be used of Canaanite gods (Gen. 35.2, 4; Judg. 10.16; I Sam. 7.3; Jer. 5.19) and, when it is clear that it is Mesopotamian gods that are thus designated, they are the gods of the patriarchal age (Josh. 24.20, 23). It might be thought that the phrase 'other gods which you (and your fathers) have not known' and its variants, common in Deuteronomy and Jeremiah, could refer to gods newly brought to the land by the Assyrians. This may indeed be true in some instances, although it can never be demonstrated. Sometimes the phrase is more closely defined as, for example, 'the gods of the peoples who are round about you, whether near to you or far from you . . .' (Deut. 13.7–8, EVV 6–7), or is linked with the names of Canaanite gods, as in Jer. 7.9: 'Baal and . . . other gods . . .' The indefinite nature of this terminology prohibits further analysis. Individual texts may be judged on their own merit, but there exist no criteria for determining when these expressions refer to Assyrian gods, let alone to officially imposed cults.

60. An attempt will be made to show that the cult of the stars in Judah was rooted in popular superstition (see ch. VI), but by the time of Manasseh's reign it was doubtless partly influenced by contact with Assyrian religious beliefs.

CHAPTER V

1. See ch. I and the various works referred to in the course of the discussion that follows here.

2. Cf. II Kings 22. For further details and discussion on this subject, see Nicholson, *Deuteronomy and Tradition*, pp. 1–36.

3. Östreicher, *op. cit.*, p. 40. He supposes that the book had a kind of moderating influence, ensuring that the reforms were extended beyond the purge of Assyrian gods.

4. Nicholson, *op. cit.*, p. 13. Nicholson gives a summary of present-day opinion on this subject on pp. 9–13.

5. Whilst the use of *wāw* with the perfect in these verses may sometimes indicate glossation (e.g., v. 4d: *wᵉnāsa' 'et-ᶜapārām bēt-'ēl*; v. 12d: *wᵉhišlīk 'et-ᶜapārām 'el-naḥal qidrōn*; cf. Stade, *ZAW* 5, pp. 291ff.), it seems unlikely that each occurrence of the construction is to be interpreted in this way, and it may often indicate that material has been inserted from a second source; cf. Budde, *art. cit.* See also ch. III, n. 5. For the suggestion that II Kings 23.4–14 derives from two sources, one dealing with an anti-Assyrian purge, see especially Östreicher, Procksch and Jepsen. (Jepsen argues that the text should be rearranged rather than divided into sources.)

6. Gressmann follows the translation of Ashurbanipal's *Annals* given by M. Streck, *Assurbanipal und die letzten assyrischen Könige bis zum Untergange Ninevehs*, VAB 7, 1916, vol.II, p.41 (see further my account on p.61), who reads 'Bêlit'. But this is a misinterpretation, for it is now known that the name of the spouse of Ashur should be read Ninlil.

7. Montgomery, *Kings*, pp.529f.

8. *KAI* 202 B 23–6; *ANET*, p.502 (early eighth century BC). That Shamash and Sahr were indigenous deities, see R. Dussaud, *Les religions des hittites et des hourites, des phéniciens et des syriens*, 'Mana': introduction à l'histoire des religions 1.2, Paris 1945, p.358.

9. Montgomery, *Kings*, p.530.

10. See also Jepsen's refutation of Gressmann (*Baumgärtel Festschrift*, pp. 100–1). But Jepsen still believes that the Host of Heaven were Assyrian gods. On this see further ch.VI below.

11. *KAI* 218.

12. The Greek names are commonly used, for example, in Philo of Byblos.

13. On these various gods, see pp.68f. On the possible |identification of Nisroch with Marduk or Nusku, see Montgomery, *Kings*, p.500; Gray, *Kings*, pp.694–5; cf. also J. P. Lettinga, 'A Note on 2 Kings xix 37', *VT* 7, 1957, pp.105–6, who argues that Nisroch is Ashur and Marduk blended into one name.

14. Östreicher, *op. cit.*, p.43.

15. Ex. 34.13; Deut. 12.3; Judg. 6.26; Micah 5.12–13, EVV 13–14; etc. See also the information collected and analysed by Patai, *art. cit.*, pp.39–41. Cf. de Vaux, *Ancient Israel*, p.286.

16. C. L. Woolley, 'The Excavation at Ur', *Antiquaries Journal* 5, London, 1925, pp.347–402, ref. p.393.

17. Lucian of Samosata, *De Dea Syria* 42 (2nd cent. AD).

18. Gressmann, *ZAW* 42, pp.325–6.

19. J. Gray, *The Legacy of Canaan*, SVT 5, Leiden, 1957, p.156.

20. Cf. B. L. Goff, 'Syncretism in the Religion of Israel', *JBL* 58, 1939, pp.151–61, ref. p.154; Montgomery, *Kings*, p.531. On different types of cult prostitutes, see B. A. Brooks, 'Fertility Cult Functionaries in the Old Testament', *JBL* 60, 1941, pp.227–53.

21. W. C. Graham and H. G. May, *Culture and Conscience. An archaeological study of the new religious past in ancient Palestine*, University of Chicago Publications in Religious Education, Chicago, 1936, p.64.

22. Ahaz's roof altars could have been dedicated either to Baal or to the Host of Heaven; see pp.9f. Manasseh is said to have erected altars to both Baal (probably the Phoenician Baal, see pp.21ff.) and to the Host of Heaven in II Kings 21.3–5. The fact that 'two courts' are mentioned in this verse need not imply that it was interpolated in the post-exilic period, as some commentators have argued. Very little is known about the courts of the pre-exilic Temple. See Parrot, *The Temple*, p.59, n.1; Gray, *Kings*, pp.706–7, 737.

23. As is argued by Östreicher, *op. cit.*, p.54.

24. See ch.VI and pp.10, 25–7.

25. Östreicher, *op. cit.*, pp.53–5.

26. See p.16 and ch.III, n.27.

27. Some examples are given in the discussion that follows on pp.32ff. and also on pp.49ff.

28. See pp.52f. and ch.VI, n.78.

29. S. H. Langdon, *Die neubabylonischen Königsinschriften*, VAB 4, 1912, p.260, line 33.

30. See, for example, Gressmann, *art. cit.*, p.323. Cf. K. Galling, 'Die Ehrenname Elisas und die Entrückung Elias', *ZThK* 53, 1956, pp.129–48, ref. p.143.

31. A. Salonen, *Die Landfahrzeuge des alten Mesopotamien*, Annales Academiae Scientiarum Fennicae, Ser.B, 72.3, Helsinki, 1951, pp.66–76.

32. *KAI* 214.2, 3, 11, 18.

33. Since the vocalization of *rkb'l* is uncertain, it may mean 'chariot (or steed) of El' or 'charioteer of El' (see *KAI* II, p.34). Either alternative equally suggests the presence of a chariot (and therefore presumably horses) in the Zinjirli mythology. This conclusion finds confirmation in the discovery of the name *rkb'l* inscribed on the pole of a chariot; cf. A. Dupont-Sommer, 'Une inscription nouvelle du roi Kilamanou et le dieu Rekoub-el', *RHR* 133, 1948, pp.19–33.

34. Unfortunately the god *rkb'l* is known only from Zinjirli, but the inscriptions belong to the mid-eighth century BC (*KAI* II, p.214) when Panammu was king of Zinjirli, probably before his submission to Assyria (*KAI* 215), and it is unlikely that his Sun-cult was influenced by Assyrian religion. Subservience to Assyria, whilst frequently referred to by Bar-rekub, Panammu's son (*KAI* 215–221), is never mentioned by Panammu himself. Bar-rekub's gods were both Syro-Phoenician and Assyrian, but Panammu's inscription shows no clear Assyrian influence at all. The Zinjirli inscriptions therefore seem to offer evidence for the separate and independent local existence in north-west Syria of an ancient mythology in which there featured a charioteer-god, *rkb'*.

35. In each instance where the gods are listed *rkb'l* is placed immediately before Shamash, possibly suggesting an intimate relationship between the two. Reshef appears as an attendant of the Sun at Ugarit; cf. *UT* 143, where he is described as 'the door-keeper (*tġr*) of Shapash'. See further Ch. Virolleaud, 'Les nouvelles tablettes de Ras Shamra', *Syria* 28, 1951, pp.22–56, ref. p.25; J. F. A. Sawyer and F. R. Stephenson, 'Literary and Astronomical Evidence for a Total Eclipse of the Sun Observed in Ancient Ugarit on 3 May 1375 B.C.', *Bulletin of the School of Oriental and African Studies, University of London* 33, 1970, pp.467–89. In Hab. 3.5 he features as an attendant of Yahweh who in vv.4, 8 is described in language reminiscent of a solar mythology (see further p.34). For a fuller discussion of the nature of this god, see D. Conrad, 'Der Gott Reshef', *ZAW* 83, 1971, pp.157–83. El may also have had solar attributes. Servius, *In Vergilii Aeneidos Commentarius* (4th cent. AD), I.642, certainly had this impression: *omnes in illis partibus solem colunt, qui ipsorum lingua El dicitur*. The solar emblem surmounts a stele from Ras Shamra which depicts the king of Ugarit making an offering to El (C. F. A. Schaeffer, *The Cuneiform Texts of Ras Shamra—Ugarit*, Schweich Lectures 1936, London, 1939, Pl.XXXI; cf. pp.61–2). It is also just possible that one of the titles of El at Ugarit, 'king, father of years', suggests that he was thought of as the

ruler of the seasons, the Sun; so it is suggested by R. Dussaud, 'La Mythologie Phénicienne', *RHR* 103–4, 1931, pp. 353–408, ref. pp. 358ff., but the title is open to other interpretations.

36. *Homeric Hymns* 2.62ff.; 4.69; 31.9 (8th—6th cent. BC); Sophocles, *Ajax* 845, 856 (5th cent. BC); Euripides, *Ion* 82 (5th cent. BC).

37. Cf. Ovid, *Metamorphoses* 2.1–503 (1st cent. AD). On the island of Rhodes, which was entirely consecrated to Helios, an annual summer festival, the *Halia*, was held in his honour. Chariot racing was a notable feature of this festival, and four consecrated horses were thrown into the sea as a sacrifice to him. Cf. W. R. Smith, *The Religion of the Semites*, p. 293.

38. McKay, *VT* 20, pp. 451–64; P. Grelot, 'Isaïe XIV 12–15 et son arrière-plan mythologique', *RHR* 149, 1956, pp. 18–48. See also p. 57 above.

39. Except in ancient India where the Sun also drove across the sky in a horse-drawn chariot (*Rig Veda* I.115.3–4; VIII.60.3; IX.63.8; cf. T. H. Gaster, *IDB* IV, pp. 463–5). But there is little evidence that Indian mythology influenced Israelite thought. Chariot mythology is found elsewhere, but not in connection with the Sun. For example, amongst the Hittites it was the Weather-god, the husband of the Sun-goddess, who rode a chariot drawn by bulls, not horses; cf. O. R. Gurney, *The Hittites*[2], Pelican Books, 1954, p. 134.

40. Schaeffer, *op. cit.*, Pl. xv.2; see fig. 2 below. Dr Schaeffer informs me that the figurines were found some metres from the chariot.

41. W. M. F. Petrie, *Gerar*, Publications of the Egyptian Research Account and the British School of Archaeology in Egypt 43, London, 1928, Pl. xxxix.12–14; see fig. 2 below.

42. *Ibid.*, Pl. xxxix.15–18; O. Tufnell, C. H. Inge and L. Harding, *Lachish II (Tell ed-Duweir): The Fosse Temple*, The Wellcome-Marston Archaeological Research Expedition to the Near East Publications 2, Oxford, 1940, Pl. xxviii.1; H. G. May and R. M. Engberg, *Material Remains of the Megiddo Cult*, The University of Chicago Oriental Institute Publications 26, Chicago, 1935, pp. 23–5; see fig. 4 below. Comparable model wheels dating from a much earlier period, from the third and second millennia BC, have also been found in Assyria and Turkestan (Petrie, *Gerar*, p. 18).

43. Whilst admitting that this is probably correct, C. C. McCown, 'Hebrew High Places and Cult Remains', *JBL* 69, 1950, pp. 205–19, points out that these chariot wheels may simply have been toys.

44. Cf. Graham and May, *op. cit.*, pp. 242–3; H. G. May, 'Some Aspects of Solar Worship at Jerusalem', *ZAW* 55, 1937, pp. 269–81, mentions (p. 271, n. 2) a Greek bronze model wheel inscribed 'to Apollo'.

45. K. M. Kenyon, 'Excavations in Jerusalem 1967', *PEQ* 1968, pp. 97–109, Pl. xxxvi.A (see fig. 5 below). Since they were found lying in a cave, they are difficult to date. ±700 BC has been suggested, allowing a fairly wide margin either way.

46. Y. Yadin and others, *Hazor III–IV*, Pl. ccclvi.1 and clxxvi.24; cf. Y. Yadin, 'The Third Season of Excavation at Hazor, 1957', *BA* 21, 1958, pp. 30–47, ref. p. 46 and fig. 16. (See fig. 6 below. But Yadin, *Hazor*, Schweich Lectures, pp. 145–6, n. 1, now thinks that this is a bull's head with a solar emblem. However, despite his further arguments, I feel that his first opinion was probably the more correct, for the most prominent feature of the bull in

ancient art, namely the horns, is lacking.) Cf. the more crude horse's (?) head with a disc on its forehead also found at Hazor; see *Hazor II*, Pl. CLXIII.11 and CIII.9. Horses' heads without discs have been found at several Palestinian sites and it is possible that these also must be considered as votive offerings to the Sun; see the comments in J. W. Crowfoot, G. M. Crowfoot and K. M. Kenyon, *Samaria–Sebaste. Reports of the work of the Joint Expedition in 1931– 1933 and of the British Expedition in 1935, no. 3. The Objects from Samaria,* London, 1957, p. 78; cf. *ibid.*, Pl. XXII and p. 77, fig. B.

47. May and Engberg, *loc. cit.*

48. Translators usually take *rekeb* in v. 11 to denote a single chariot and in v. 12 to be a collective noun meaning 'chariotry'; *pārāšāw* in v. 12 is frequently translated 'its horsemen', rather than 'its horses' (e.g. RSV; NEB; Gray, *Kings*, p. 473; Montgomery, *Kings*, p. 354; M. A. Beek, 'The Meaning of the Expression "The Chariots and Horsemen of Israel" (II Kings ii 12)', *The Witness of Tradition: papers read at the joint British-Dutch Old Testament Conference held at Woudschoten, 1970*, OTS 17, 1972, pp. 1–10). But a number of scholars now feel that *pārāš* means 'horse', not 'horseman' (e.g. K. Galling, *art. cit.*, pp. 131–5; D. R. Ap-Thomas, 'All the King's Horses; a study of the term פרשׁ (I Kings 5.6 [EVV, 4.26] etc.)', *Proclamation and Presence. Old Testament Essays in Honour of Gwynne Henton Davies*, ed. J. I. Durham and J. R. Porter, London, 1970, pp. 135–51), and *rekeb* may equally well be translated 'chariot' in both verses. LXX and Vg suggest the reading *pārāšō*.

49. The phrase recurs in II Kings 13.14 where it appears to be a title for Elisha. Hence it is usually interpreted in 2.12 as a title for Elijah. In the context it may therefore be expressive of the prophet's charismatic qualities. Nevertheless, it would not have been used in the first instance unless the allusion was recognizable from its mythological background as an expression of divine power.

50. Beek, *art. cit.*, maintains that the background is theological and that the phrase is descriptive of the power of Yahweh as manifested in the Exodus and other historical events in which the chariotry of Israel's foes and oppressors was seen to be no match for the might of Yahweh whose divine force was therefore well described as 'horses and chariots of fire'; cf. particularly II Kings 6.17. Beek points to a number of passages which may support his claim about the chariot imagery in the Old Testament, but his arguments about the connection with fire in the Elijah-Elisha narratives do not appear to be so well founded. The fire that kindles the wood for sacrifice on Mount Carmel (I Kings 18.24) and the destructive fire of judgment (II Kings 1.10–14) are hardly to be regarded as the same phenomena as the fire of Yahweh's chariotry arranged for war on Elisha's behalf (II Kings 6.13–17) or the fire of the chariot(s) which separated Elijah and Elisha (II Kings 2.11). Again, there does not seem to be a very close similarity between chariots of fire which cover the hills around Elisha, a whole vast heavenly army (II Kings 6.13–17), and the presumably more compact manifestation which separated the two prophets as they walked side by side (II Kings 2.11). The imagery, it appears, must be interpreted in its contexts and the same interpretation may not be applicable in each instance. No doubt to the Israelite the chariot of fire motif may have conveyed little more than the impression of divine power, but it is

also not unlikely that this motif finds its origin in the concept of a solar deity mounted on a chariot.

51. Cf. W. F. Albright, 'The Psalm of Habakkuk', *Studies in Old Testament Prophecy presented to Professor T. H. Robinson*, ed. H. H. Rowley, Edinburgh, 1950, pp. 1–18. But contrast W. A. Irwin, 'The Psalm of Habakkuk', *JNES* 1, 1942, pp. 10–40, and 'The Mythological Background of Habakkuk, Chapter 3', *JNES* 15, 1956, pp. 47–50, who believes that the Babylonian *Enuma Elish* provided the background to Hab. 3.

52. RV: 'upon thy chariots of salvation',
RSV: 'upon thy chariot of victory',
Jer. Bib.: 'on your victorious chariots',
NEB: 'thy riding is to victory'.
BH³ and BHS both suggest emendation of the text and the translation 'chariot' adopted here presupposes their proposed reading, *merkabteka*.

53. So S. R. Driver, *The Minor Prophets II: Nahum, Habakkuk, Zephaniah, Haggai, Zechariah, Malachi*, CB, 1906, pp. 90–1; G. W. Wade, *The Book of the Prophet Habakkuk*, WC, 1929, p. 202.

54. See above, n. 35. NEB, RSV translate 'plague'.

55. Dhorme, *Religions*, pp. 61–2; Tallqvist, *Der assyrische Gott*, pp. 106–11. The winged solar disc was not Mesopotamian in origin and was by no means peculiar to Assyria. It was also known in Hatti, Egypt, Syro-Phoenicia and even in Judah where it appears on the *lmlk* jar-handle stamps of the seventh century BC. The Judaean examples, however, show no Mesopotamian influence, but are most closely akin in style to the Syro-Phoenician forms; see A. D. Tushingham, 'A Royal Israelite Seal (?) and the Royal Jar Handle Stamps (Part Two)', *BASOR* 201, 1971, pp. 23–35. Thus, whilst the Israelite also knew of a winged Sun-disc, he appears to have been little influenced by Mesopotamian solar art and mythology. Hence the preservation in Israel of an ancient tradition about a Sun-god who journeyed by horse-drawn chariot must be entirely independent of Mesopotamian influences. See further, pp. 52f. and fig. 13b below.

56. As, for example, the theory proposed by C. H. Gordon, *Before the Bible. The Common Background of Greek and Hebrew Civilizations*, London, 1962.

57. S. R. Driver, 'Parbar', *HDB* III, p. 673.

58. *KAI* 260 B 3, 5.

59. Östreicher, *op. cit.*, p. 54, believed that this was a very strong argument for the presence of Assyrian solar worship in Jerusalem. Cf. also Gressmann, *ZAW* 42, p. 323.

60. So *K-B*, p. 776.

61. A. S. Yahuda, 'Hebrew Words of Egyptian Origin', *JBL* 66, 1947, pp. 83–90, ref. p. 88.

62. Gressmann, *art. cit.*, p. 326. In order to maintain this conclusion he was obliged to omit v. 5b from the text.

63. LXX and Pesh read singular; MT reads plural. For the suggestion that these priests were the officials of a solar cult at Bethel, see F. J. Hollis, 'The Sun Cult and the Temple at Jerusalem', *Myth and Ritual. Essays on the myth and ritual of the Hebrews in relation to the culture pattern of the ancient East*, ed. S. H. Hooke, London, 1933, pp. 87–110.

64. Montgomery, *Kings*, pp. 538-9.

65. Van Driel, *The Cult of Aššur*, p. 175; *AHw*, p. 506; *CAD*, vol. K, pp. 534-5 (it is also found in the Mari texts).

66. Cf. Snaith, *Kings*, p. 321.

67. See above, n. 63.

68. *KAI* 225.1; 226.1.

69. W. F. Albright, *From the Stone Age to Christianity. Monotheism and the Historical Process*[2], Doubleday Anchor Books, New York, 1957, pp. 234f., thinks that in Western Semitic world the term *kōmer* denoted 'male prostitute' or 'eunuch priest'; on the close association of the *bāmōt* with fertility religion, see above ch. IV, n. 6.

70. See pp. 45ff., 50 and n. 77 below.

71. See p. 30.

72. Cf. pp. 30f.

73. *BDB*, p. 1039; *K-B*, p. 995.

74. See further L. I. J. Stadelmann, *The Hebrew Conception of the World, a philological and literary study*, AnBib 39, 1970, pp. 63ff., 75ff.

75. *CAD*, vol. Aii, pp. 259ff.; K. Tallqvist, *Akkadische Götterepitheta*, SO 7, 1938, pp. 442-8.

76. See above, n. 69, and ch. IV, n. 6.

77. A tablet from Ras Shamra celebrates the marriage of the Canaanite *yrḫ* to the Mesopotamian *nkl* (*CML*, pp. 124-7 = *CTCA*, 24) and it has been noted that both *yrḫ* and *nkl* feature as fertility deities in this poem. (Cf. T. H. Gaster, 'The "Graces" in Semitic Folklore', *JRAS* 1938, pp. 37-56; C. H. Gordon, 'A Marriage of the Gods in Canaanite Mythology', *BASOR* 65, 1937, pp. 29-33.) Similarly, *špš* in Ugaritic mythology aids Anat in her attempt to restore Baal to his throne, thus assisting in the renovation of fertility on earth (*CML*, B I i.11ff. = *CTCA*, 6 I.11ff.; cf. A. Caquot, 'La divinité solaire ougaritique', *Syria* 36, 1959, pp. 90-101). See also p. 50.

78. Shamash had other aspects as well, e.g., that of war-god, but of these that of vegetation god was the least significant. Cf. Tallqvist, *Götterepitheta*, pp. 453-60; *GMVO*, pp. 126-7; Dhorme, *Religions*, pp. 60-7.

79. In late Hebrew writing *mazzālōt* is used of both constellations and planets; in Aramaic *mazzālā* denotes not only constellations and planets, but their influence on the fate of men (cf. Mod. Heb.); in Syriac both *mawzaltā* and *mazlē* are found with the meanings 'Zodiac' and 'stations of the Moon' respectively; the Arabs used *manāzilu* of the Zodiac or the stations of the Moon; on a bilingual Phoenician inscription the phrase [*mz*]*l n'm* is found together with the translation ἀγαθῇ τύχῃ; and the Accadian *mazzaztu* or *manzaztu* (var. *manzaltu*, late Babylonian; *mazzaltu*, middle Assyrian) means 'position', 'post', 'station', but is used, amongst a variety of different ways, to mean 'station' of siderial gods, while *mazzāzu* or *manzāzu*, again amongst other things, may mean 'station' or 'stand' of gods, stars, planets, lunar phases and constellations. Full details and discussion of these terms may be found in the following: *BDB*, p. 561; *K-B*, p. 509 (cf. also *Supplementum* to *K-B*, p. 165); W. Gesenius, *Thesaurus Philologicus Criticus Linguae Hebraeae et Chaldaeae Veteris Testamenti*, Lipsiae, 1835-58, *ad loc.*; G. V. Schiaparelli, *Astronomy in the Old Testament*, Oxford, 1905; E. W. Maunder, *The Astronomy*

of the Bible: an elementary commentary on the astronomical references of Holy Scripture[3], London, 1909; M. A. Stern, 'Die Sternbilder in Hiob 38.31–2', *Geiger's Jüdische Zeitschrift* 3, pp. 258–76 (not available to me; cited and summarized by Schiaparelli, *op. cit.*, pp. 163–75); G. R. Driver, 'Two Astronomical Passages in the Old Testament', *JTS* NS 4, 1953, pp. 208–12; Stadelmann, *op. cit.*, pp. 85ff.; *AHw*, p. 638.

80. The Versions are confused in II Kings 23.5 and Job 38.32. In both cases LXX transliterates (μαζουρώθ); Vg translates *duodecim signa* and *Lucifer* respectively; Pesh renders *mawzaltā* (zodiac) and *ʿgeltā* (chariot).

81. Stern: the Hyades,
    Schiaparelli: Venus-Ishtar,
    Maunder: the Zodiac,
    Gesenius: *duodecim signa*,
    Driver, Stadelmann: the (five) planets,
    BDB, K-B: constellations, or signs of the Zodiac,
    Jewish scholars: (variously) the Zodiac, Corona Borealis, the belt of Orion.

82. The Zodiac is first evidenced in Mesopotamia on a tablet dated 419 BC and it appears that it had then been fairly recently determined; cf. A. Sachs, 'Babylonian Horoscopes', *JCS* 6, 1952, pp. 49–75, ref. p. 52; B. L. van der Waerden, 'Babylonian Astronomy I. The History of the Zodiac', *AfO* 16, 1942–3, pp. 216–30. O. Neugebauer, *The Exact Sciences in Antiquity*[2], Providence, 1957, ch. 5, maintains that its invention results from the growing need for an exact frame of reference as the Babylonian astronomers turned more to mathematical computation and measurement; cf. Sachs, *loc. cit.*, on the similar needs of the astrologers.

83. See above, n. 79.

84. It is precisely because there is no evidence that the Zodiac was worshipped that G. R. Driver, *art. cit.*, preferred to identify the *mazzālōt* with the five planets.

85. *AHw*, pp. 124, 421, 638; see also above, n. 79.

86. It is usually suggested that these are alternative spellings of the same word, since *r* and *l* are often interchangeable in Semitic languages; cf. BDB, p. 561; Stadelmann, *op. cit.*, pp. 85ff.; but contrast Driver, *art. cit.*

87. *Pace* Stadelmann, *loc. cit.*, who thinks *mazzārōt* is a planet, but planets do not have seasons; only individual stars and constellations have seasons for rising and setting. The masculine singular suffix of *bᵉittō* also implies that *mazzārōt*, despite the feminine plural termination, refers to one single constellation. It also rules out any identification with Ishtar/Astarte/Venus who was a goddess. Certainly Venus was a male god in Arabia, but the Arabs used the word *manāzilu* to designate the stations of the Moon.

88. This suggestion implies that, if *mazzālōt/mazzārōt* is an Accadian loan-word (so M. Ellenbogen, *Foreign Words in the Old Testament, their origin and etymology*, London 1962, p. 100), it was taken into Hebrew with a meaning rather different from the Accadian equivalent in the first instance.

89. Gray, *Kings*, p. 730, reading *bēt haśśōʿᵃrīm* (shrine of the gate-genii) for MT's *bāmōt haśśᵉʿārīm* (high-places of the gates).

90. Reading *bāmat haśśᵉʿīrīm*; cf. G. Hoffmann, 'Kleinigkeiten', *ZAW* 2,

1882, p. 175. Satyrs were creatures, probably demonic, of the waste and desert land, and are listed by Isaiah along with wild-beasts, howling creatures, ostriches, jackals, hyenas and the night hag (Isa. 13.21–2; 34.14–RSV). Presumably the cult was therefore centred on the worship of some such demon of the Palestinian wastes and was rooted in popular superstitious fear of dark and unseen forces.

91. *Tōpet* is perhaps not a place name, but a common noun meaning 'furnace' or 'fire-pit', since it is pointed with the vowels of *bōšet* (shame) and bears the definite article; cf. *BDB*, p. 1075; W. R. Smith, *op. cit.*, p. 377. It has also been argued that *hinnōm* was not a proper name, but a descriptive noun meaning 'resting place (of the dead)', from the verb *nūm*, 'to sleep' (P. Haupt, 'Hinnom and Kidron', *JBL* 38, 1919, pp. 45–8; but contrast Jer. 7.32 where the Hinnom Valley is certainly not a graveyard). Thus the *bᵉnē-hinnōm* (so *Kᵉtib*, but *Qᵉrē*, the Versions and many MSS read singular) may have been a sect (cf. the personal name, *hnmy*, found on a Judean seal; Montgomery, *Kings*, p. 539) that gathered in the place of the dead to perform rites. But traditionally *hinnōm* is the name of a place (later Gehenna) located in the Kidron Valley. See further Montgomery, *Kings*, p. 532; Gray, *Kings*, pp. 735–6.

92. O. Eissfeldt, *Molk als Opferbegriff im Punischen und Hebräischen und das Ende des Gottes Moloch*, Beiträge zur Religionsgeschichte des Altertums 3, Halle 1935.

93. Ch. Virolleaud, 'Les nouvelles tablettes alphabétiques de Ras Shamra', *CRAI* 1956, pp. 60–67; H. Cazelles, 'Molok', *Supplément au Dictionnaire de la Bible* V, Paris, 1957, cols 1337–46, ref. cols. 1339, 1345.

94. S. H. Langdon, *Semitic Mythology*, The Mythology of All Races 5, Boston 1931, p. 50; P. Jensen, 'Die Götter כמוש und מלך und die Erscheinungsformen *Kammuš* und *Malik* des assyrisch-babylonischen Gottes *Nergal*', *ZA* 42, 1934, pp. 235–7; Albright, *Archaeology and the Religion of Israel*, pp. 162–4.

95. Cazelles, *art. cit.*, cols. 1343ff.; cf. Eissfeldt, *op. cit.*, pp. 43–4.

96. So with variations Lev. 18.21; Deut. 18.10; II Kings 16.3; 21.6; Jer. 32.35.

97. So E. Dhorme, Review of O. Eissfeldt, *Molk als Opferbegriff*, *RHR* 113, 1936, pp. 276–8; cf. N. H. Snaith, 'The Cult of Molech', *VT* 16, 1966, pp. 123–4, who compares the Molech rite with the making of a Covenant by passing between two parts of a sacrificial victim and suggests that its purpose was the dedication of children to be brought up as cult prostitutes.

98. Deut. 12.31; II Kings 17.31; Jer. 7.31; 19.5. However, it has been suggested recently that even this verb need not be taken literally, but that it may signify a rite of consecration associated with the god Adad (M. Weinfeld, *Deuteronomy and the Deuteronomic School*, Oxford 1972, p. 216, n. 1). Comparison is made with the similar use of the word *šarāpu* in the phrase to 'burn the first son' in some Neo-Assyrian texts where the meaning, it seems, is not literal, but refers to a rite of consecration in which the burning of spices played an important part. Then, on the grounds that II Kings 17.30 mentions Adad-melek (MT reads '*adrammelek*) as a god to whom the men of Sepharvaim burned their children, it is argued that the Judaean Molech rite may be compared with the Assyrian ceremony. However, apart from the uncertainty of

the emendation required to obtain the reading *'adadmelek* (for an alternative suggestion see Gray, *Kings*, p. 655), II Kings 17.30 suggests that the cult of the Sepharvites is not so easily defined. Their rite is said to have honoured not one, but two deities, Adrammelek and Anammelek, and since both names are conflate with *mlk*, it seems more likely that the cult of these gods reflects some kind of syncretism with Palestinian Molech worship than that it was an entirely Assyrian importation (see also ch. VIII, n. 12). It would therefore be hazardous to base an equation of the Molech rite in Judah with elements in the worship of the Assyrian Adad on this text. Furthermore, it is doubtful whether the people of Judah, who could hardly have been ignorant of Phoenician child-sacrifice and to whom the verb *śārap* meant precisely 'to burn', would have used the phrase *leśerōp 'et-benēhēm we'et-benōtēhem bā'ēš* if it did not mean child sacrifice by burning in fire.

99. See p. 7 and ch. II, n. 10.

100. Cf. Eissfeldt, *op. cit.*, pp. 46–65.

101. See ch. II, n. 45. See also the comment of Curtius Rufus, quoted above, ch. II, n. 51.

102. D. Harden, *The Phoenicians*, Ancient Peoples and Places, London 1962, pp. 94–5; Diodorus Siculus, *Bibliotheca Historica* I xx.14; Curtius Rufus, *loc. cit.*

103. Cf. Deut. 12.31; 18.9–10; II Kings 16.3.

104. Cf. Lev. 20.2–5: to indulge in the Molech cult is 'to defile my sanctuary and profane my holy name'. The immediate implication of this text is that the cult was practised at a Yahweh-shrine, but it could also be that the expression is little more than a pietistic description of the perversion of Yahwism by those who remained worshippers of the god of Israel and also took part in the Molech cult.

105. If the Old Testament Molech is to be associated with the Phoenician word *mlk*, then it is perhaps relevant that in Latin inscriptions substitution sacrifice to Saturn is described as *magnum sacrificium nocturnum molchomor* (or *morchomor*, cf. Phoenician *mlk'mr*; Eissfeldt, *op. cit.*, pp. 1–7; J. Carcopino, 'Survivances par Substitution des Sacrifices d'Enfants dans l'Afrique Romaine', *RHR* 106, 1932, pp. 592–9). Alternatively, if any connection with the Mesopotamian Malik is allowed (see pp. 40f.), then it is possible to suggest an astral aspect since Malik was identified with Nergal (Tallqvist, *Götterepitheta*, p. 359) who had a secondary association with the planet Mars (see p. 48). There is no direct evidence in the Old Testament to the effect that the Molech cult had any astral connection, but J. Gray, 'The Desert God 'AṬTR in the Literature and Religion of Canaan', *JNES* 8, 1949, pp. 72–83, has argued that Molech is to be identified with Athtar-Venus. However, this identification does not appear to have a very firm basis. It depends on the identification of Molech with Milkom in I Kings 11.7, but the text here may be corrupt, for LXX reads τῷ βασιλεῖ αὐτῶν which is elsewhere a common translation of *Milkōm*. The translators, having an unpointed text, read the word as *malkām* (cf. I Kings 11.5, 33; Zeph. 1.5), but if this is so, their text contained no allusion to a god Molech (see also A. Caquot, 'Le dieu 'Aṭtr et les textes de Ras Shamra', *Syria* 35, 1958, pp. 45–60, and ch. VI, n. 36 below). Nevertheless, it is perhaps noteworthy that the Molech cult is closely associated with the

astral cults in Jer. 7.31—8.3; 19.10–13; II Kings 23.10–12. Thus it is possible that the Hinnom rites did honour an astral deity, who may have been some manifestation of Baal (cf. Jer. 2.23; 19.5; 32.35), perhaps similar; to Baʿal-Ḥammōn, the Phoenician god of North Africa to whom children were sacrificed as in the Hinnom Valley and whom the Greeks identified with Kronos-Saturn (*GMVO*, pp. 271f.); cf. K. Budde, 'The Sabbath and the Week', *JTS* 30, 1928, pp. 1–15, who argued on different grounds that Israel learned the worship of Saturn from the Kenites.

106. The cults of Kemosh, Milkom and Ashtoreth shared a common locality, perhaps even a common *bāmā* (I Kings 11.7 reads singular; LXX of II Kings 23.13 suggests *habbayit*). Community of locality, it is argued, suggests community of nature and of cult, and the three deities were certainly national gods and war-gods, possibly even local manifestations of the same (astral?) god. Further support for this opinion is adduced by noting that Judg. 11.24 suggests the equation of Kemosh and Milkom and that the Moabite Stone (line 17) presents the compound name Ashtar-Kemosh. J. B. Curtis, 'An Investigation of the Mount of Olives in Judaeo-Christian Tradition', *HUCA* 28, 1957, pp. 137–80, argues that these gods should be commonly associated with Mars, and J. Gray, *JNES* 8, pp. 72–83, proposes an equation with Athtar-Venus, but the question of exact identity is fraught with dubiety. A good case can be made for finding astral qualities in Kemosh and Ashtoreth (see p. 51 and ch. VI, n. 65), but very little is known about Milkom.

107. It is sometimes considered extensive, sometimes slight. See recently H. D. Lance, 'The Royal Stamp and the Kingdom of Josiah', *HTR* 64, 1971, pp. 315–32. This, however, is a subject for study elsewhere.

108. On *'ōb* and *yiddeʿōnī*, and on the subject of divination in Israel, see p. 58 and ch. VI, n. 115. *Terāpîm, gillulîm* and *šiqquṣîm* were probably various kinds of idols, but *terāpîm* were known in Israel from earliest times (e.g., I Sam. 19.13, 16) and the other two terms are used by the Deuteronomist himself to describe idols in Israel well before the advent of the Assyrians (I Kings 15.12; 11.5, 7).

109. That is, accepting that Jeremiah's ministry began about 627 BC (cf. Jer. 1.2; 25.3). For a good comprehensive outline and discussion of the reasons why various scholars have found this date difficult, and for a statement of the position accepted here, see T. W. Overholt, 'Some Reflections on the Date of Jeremiah's Call', *CBQ* 33, 1971, pp. 165–84. The date of Zephaniah's ministry has also been questioned; cf. J. P. Hyatt, 'The Date and Background of Zephaniah', *JNES* 7, 1948, pp. 25–9; L. P. Smith and E. R. Lacheman, 'The Authorship of the Book of Zephaniah', *JNES* 9, 1950, pp. 137–42; D. L. Williams, 'The Date of Zephaniah', *JBL* 82, 1963, pp. 77–88.

110. My own opinion on this matter, which I hope to discuss more fully at some future date (see also pp. 70ff. and ch. VIII, n. 13), is that the reformation, though greatly aided by the spirit of the age, was primarily motivated by the religious zeal and determination of the people who stood behind the law-book, namely the Deuteronomists. These I see as a mixed group of people, originally refugees from the North after 722 BC, who lived and worked among the 'people of the land', making converts among its more influential

figures. This reforming movement, probably comprising men from all walks of life and different circles within society, having thus gained leaders of status, used the opportunity offered at the accession of Josiah by a period of regency to put their programme of reform into operation. The reformation was thus essentially Deuteronomic from beginning to end.

CHAPTER VI

1. This covers a large amount of Old Testament scripture: Hosea, Micah, Isaiah of Jerusalem, Jeremiah, Zephaniah, Nahum, Habakkuk, Ezekiel, Deuteronomy, the D-history (Joshua, Judges, I & II Samuel, I & II Kings), Lamentations, many Psalms, possibly the editing of J and E, and perhaps much else, including parts of II Chronicles which deal with this period.

2. MT reads m^eleket $ha\check{s}\check{s}\bar{a}mayim$, which suggests something like 'the workmanship of heaven' and could therefore have been a synonym for 'Host of Heaven'. Hence $m^ele'ket$ is the reading in 44.17 given by 30 MSS and in 7.18 by 52 MSS. LXX translates ἡ στρατία τοῦ οὐρανοῦ in 7.18. But the consonantal spelling in MT requires the pointing $malkat$, which is the generally accepted reading. It is supported by Aquila, Symmachus, Theodotion and Vg in 7.18 and by LXX and Vg in 44.17.

3. So Jerome; see A. Condamin, *Le livre de Jérémie*[3], Études Bibliques 12, Paris 1936, p.69.

4. So M. J. Dahood, *Revista Biblica* 8, 1960, pp.166–8 (not available to me; cited by J. Bright, *Jeremiah*[2], AB 21, 1965, p.56).

5. Tallqvist, *Götterepitheta*, pp.239–40; cf. the Sumerian Inanna, whose name means precisely 'Queen of Heaven' (A. Falkenstein, *Die Inschriften Gudeas von Lagaš I, Einleitung*, AnOr 30, 1966, pp.78f.; *GMVO*, pp.81ff.).

6. *GMVO*, p.172. 'Queen of Heaven' was also a component of the titles of the Sun-goddess of Arinna (see p.49).

7. Twelfth century BC; cf. *ANET*, p.249; J. Gray, 'Queen of Heaven', *IDB* III, p.975. Gray, who also sees difficulties in the identification of the Palestinian Queen of Heaven with the Mesopotamian Ishtar, maintains that the Venus-star, with which Ishtar was identified, was regarded as a male deity in Palestine, but we do not know enough about Palestinian astral lore to justify the conclusion that this was always the case. (See further, McKay, *VT* 20, pp.451–64.)

8. 1050–850 BC; May, *Megiddo*, pp.6f. (see fig. 7 below). With this may be compared the bird and star symbol discussed on p.55. The star from *El-Jib* is also a hexagram, though more perfect in symmetry.

9. F. J. Bliss and R. A. S. Macalister, *Excavations in Palestine during the years 1898–1900*, London 1902, Pl. 67.15s. See fig. 8 below.

10. Macalister, *Gezer* II, p.442, fig. 524. See fig. 9 below.

11. It is probably the same motif of a star in the field and a lion with a star on it shoulder that appears on a golden cup from Ras Shamra (Schaeffer, *Ras Shamra—Ugarit*, Pl. XVII and p.22, fig. 6; see fig. 10 below). The religious significance of the star on the lion's shoulder has been a recent subject of de-

bate. D. M. A. Bate, 'The "Shoulder Ornament" of Near Eastern Lions', *JNES* 9, 1950, pp. 53–4, argues that it has no religious significance, but most scholars would not agree with her conclusion; cf. H. J. Kantor, 'The Shoulder Ornament of the Near Eastern Lions', *JNES* 6, 1947, pp. 250–67; A. J. Arkell, 'The Shoulder Ornament of the Near Eastern Lions', *JNES* 7, 1948, p. 52; A. Vollgraff-Roes, 'The Lion with Body Markings in Oriental Art', *JNES* 12, 1953, pp. 40–9.

12. It is difficult to determine when Regulus was first recognized as a 'King Star'. The name 'Regulus' is medieval, but the astrologer Geminus (1st cent. BC) refers to it as ὁ βασιλίσκος and the elder Pliny (1st cent. AD) uses the words *stella regia*. Prior to this date, there is no evidence that the notion of royalty was associated with Regulus in the Graeco-Roman world where the star was given various names such as 'the bright star of Leo' or 'the star in the breast/heart' (see Pauly-Wissowa 12, 1925, cols. 1976–7). In Mesopotamian astronomy the title ^{mul} LUGAL, 'King Star', is used, but it seems that this is sometimes to be rendered Ḫaniš and is therefore not always to be regarded as an attribution of royalty. It appears, however, that most scholars think of two separate stars, one known as Ḫaniš (α Centauri is suggested) and the other as the 'King Star', namely Regulus (see F. Gössmann, *Planetarium Babylonicum oder die sumerisch-babylonischen Stern-Namen*, Šumerisches Lexikon 4.2, ed. A. Deimel, Scripta Pontificii Instituti Biblici, Rome, 1950, pp. 89–91). In India Regulus was known as *magha*, 'The Mighty' (P. Lum, *The Stars in our Heaven; myths and fables*, London 1951, p. 167).

The Lion is more firmly fixed in ancient astral lore. In Greece it was ὁ Λέων (Pauly-Wissowa 12, col. 1974), in Mesopotamia it was ^{mul}ur-*gu-la* or ^{mul}ur-*a*, the 'Great Dog' or the 'Lion' (Gössmann, *op. cit.*, pp. 64–7), and at *Qorai*š in North Arabia it was *al-'asad*, 'the Lion' (A. Grohmann, *Arabien*, Handbuch der Altertumswissenschaft 3.1.3, Kulturgeschichte des alten Orients 3.4, Munich 1963, p. 81). Thus it seems fairly clear that recognition of the astral lion and of Regulus (although not always known as the 'King Star') was widespread in the ancient world and by no means limited to Mesopotamia.

13. W. Hartner, 'The Earliest History of the Constellations in the Near East and the Motif of the Lion-Bull Combat', *JNES* 24, 1965, pp. 1–16.

14. Allowing for the precession of the equinoxes, its heliacal setting and rising respectively in the Mesopotamian – Southern Mediterranean parallel about 1000 BC would have been at the end of June and the end of July, as in Greece several hundred years later. Cf. Aratus of Soli, *Phaenomena et Diosemea* 147–51 (3rd cent. BC); see further Pauly-Wissowa 12, col. 1974. This association with the Sun at its height may have been one of the original reasons why Regulus received the title 'King Star'.

15. Schaeffer, *op. cit.*, p. 49, fig. 10. The coiffure, as on the *Tell eṣ-Ṣāfi* plaque, shows Egyptian artistic influence and again the serpent motif is present. See fig. 11 below.

16. On the antiquity of this conception, see M. Rostovetzeff, 'Dieux et chevaux', *Syria* 12, 1931, pp. 48–57, who argues that the idea of depicting the goddess on the back of a lion probably originated in Hatti or Mitanni and spread from there to Mesopotamia and Syria.

17. In Greece the mother-goddess was identified with the zodiacal constel-

lation, Virgo (Aratus, *Phaenomena* 96–146) and was associated with the mythical golden age, while her star, Spica, was known as Προτρυγητήρ, 'the Announcer of the Grape-harvest'. (In Babylonia a similar association of Virgo with harvest is seen in the name $^{mul}ab\text{-}sin$, 'the Furrow' (of corn); see Gössmann, *op. cit.*, p.3; E. F. Weidner, 'Fixsterne', *RA* III, pp.72–82). The astral associations between the mother-goddess and the lion may therefore have been suggested from the fact that Leo immediately precedes Virgo in the annual cycle of the stars.

18. In support for the argument that the cult of the Queen of Heaven was an Assyrian imposition it has been pointed out that one of the features of her worship to which Jeremiah alludes, the baking of cakes as offerings to the goddess (Jer. 7.18; 44.19), is paralleled in the worship of Ishtar (Condamin, *Jérémie*, pp.69–70). The word for 'cakes' here, *kawwānīm*, is not used elsewhere in the Old Testament and is usually held to be an Accadian loan-word, *kamānu* (so Condamin, *loc. cit.*; K-B, p.428; *AHw*, p.430). However, this argument is far from conclusive. Firstly, the practice itself was not alien to the ritual of Palestinian fertility religion. David distributed cakes of bread (*ḥallat leḥem*) and raisin cakes (*^{a}šīšā*) among the people at the end of what may have been a fertility ritual (II Sam. 6.19; cf. J. R. Porter, 'The Interpretation of 2 Samuel VI and Psalm cxxxII', *JTS* NS 5, 1954, pp.161–73), Hosea condemned Israel's paganism and her passion for raisin-cakes (*^{a}šīšē ^{a}nābīm*, 3.1), Isaiah mocked Moab's addiction to raisin-cakes (*^{a}šīšīm*, 16.7), and plaques and figurines found at various Palestinian sites portray the mother-goddess holding what are probably just such raisin-cakes (cf. Macalister, *Gezer* III, Pl.ccxxI.2; May, *Megiddo*, Pl.xxvII; *ANEP*, Pl.469; see fig. 12 below). Secondly, whilst it is possible that *kamānu* was borrowed as *kawwān*, and whilst its use here may signify some kind of Mesopotamian influence on the cult of the mother-goddess in Judah (*kamānu* was used in the cult of Ishtar, but also in the cult of Tammuz), as is naturally to be expected in this age, this does not necessitate the conclusion that the cult itself entered Palestine in the Assyrian period as part of Judah's obligation to worship the gods of her overlord. Indeed, it would be extremely difficult to establish such a conclusion from a comparison of these Hebrew and Accadian words, partly because *kawwān* is virtually a *hapax legomenon* and it is not known whether it was used exclusively in Israel in the context of the cult of the Queen of Heaven, and partly because the Accadian passages collected in *CAD*, vol.K, pp.110–1, suggest that *kamānu* in Mesopotamia was more a secular than a cultic word.

19. The exact identity of the Queen of Heaven must remain undecided, for on the basis of the information we possess she could be identified with almost any of the ancient Near Eastern goddesses who feature in mythology and art as the mother-goddess. If there was any connection between the diaspora in Egypt (Jer. 44) and the colony at Elephantine, it may be possible to recognize in the Queen of Heaven the goddess Anat (cf. the Bethshan stele) who later became Yahweh's consort. Although A. Vincent, *Religion des judéo-araméens d'Éléphantine*, pp.359ff., dates the foundation of the colony in the reign of Psammetichus I (663–609 BC), a later date is frequently favoured, possibly in the reign of Apries (588–66 BC; cf. Albright, *Archaeology and the Religion of Israel*, p.168). It is also possible that 'Queen of Heaven' was especially recog-

nized as a local title of Anat at Anathoth, Jeremiah's birth-place (Jer. 1.1), which would explain why the title was never used elsewhere in the Old Testament. Such suggestions, however, can be little more than conjectures.

It is also difficult to determine precisely when the cult flourished and when it was discontinued. Although Jer. 26.1 dates the Temple sermon 'in the beginning of the reign of Jehoiakim', it has been argued that the original setting of Jer. 7.17-18 was in the period before Josiah's reformation (C. C. Torrey, *Pseudo-Ezekiel*, pp. 45-57; *idem*, 'The Background of Jer. 1-10', *JBL* 56, 1937, pp. 193-216), and if this argument is accepted, it is possible to maintain that the worship of the Queen of Heaven may have been terminated as a result of the reforms themselves. On the other hand, if the date given in Jer. 26.1 is correct, it may have been Jeremiah's own teaching that effected the cessation. However, if the conclusion is correct that the worship of the Queen of Heaven was part of common Palestinian paganism, no doubt this cult had been in existence in some form or other for many centuries, but became particularly popular during the decline in religion following Ahaz's submission to Assyria.

20. Montgomery, *Kings*, p. 520.

21. O. Neugebauer, *The Exact Sciences in Antiquity*, ch. 5; *idem*, 'The Survival of Babylonian Methods in the Exact Sciences of Antiquity and Middle Ages'; *Proceedings of the American Philosophical Society* 107, 1963, pp. 528-35.

22. Particularly from the reign of Nabu-nasir (747-734 BC) when the Babylonians began to keep records of eclipses. See further, Neugebauer, *op. cit.*, ch. 5.

23. E.g., the astrological collections in *Enuma Anu Enlil*; see Ch. Virolleaud, *L'Astrologie Chaldéenne*, Paris 1903-12. Mesopotamian astrology at this date was not horoscopy in the modern sense of the technique of predicting an individual's future. It was still directed to determining the future of the nation's welfare and as such was not the mathematical art that it later became. See further Sachs, *JCS* 6 pp. 49-75.

24. T. Jacobsen, 'Formative Tendencies in Sumerian Religion', *The Bible and the Ancient Near East. Essays in honour of W. F. Albright*, ed. G. E. Wright, London 1961, pp. 267-78.

25. Tallqvist, *Götterepitheta*, pp. 442-8, 453-60, 330-38; *GMVO* pp. 101-3, 126-7, 81-6; Dhorme, *Religions*, pp. 53-94.

26. Tallqvist, *Götterepitheta*, pp. 389-96, 421-27; E. von Weiher, *Der babylonische Gott Nergal*, Alter Orient und Altes Testament; Veröffentlichungen zur Kultur und Geschichte des alten Orients und des Alten Testaments 11, Neukirchen-Vluyn, 1971, pp. 76ff.; see also herein, p. 68. These associations do not, however, imply that such gods were star-gods. W. G. Lambert has reminded me that, though some texts assign stars to gods, other texts assign numbers to the major deities and yet other texts assign animals and birds to various gods. Assyro-Babylonian religion was not therefore totemism.

27. Oppenheim, *art. cit.*, AnBib 12.

28. Cf. Gen. 1.14-19; Ps. 104.19, where the Sun, Moon and stars are described as marking off the seasons, and Amos 5.8-9; Job 9.9; 37.9; 38.12–

15, 31–3, where the writers select for mention some of the major constellations that had a connection with the agricultural seasons. See further G. R. Driver, *art. cit., JTS* NS 4, 1953, pp. 208–12, and NS 7, 1956, pp. 1–11.

29. See p. 58.

30. There are certain further passages in the Jeremiah prose which may suggest that the kings were as much involved in this cult – and also the cult of the Queen of Heaven – as were the people. For example, Jer. 8.1; 19.13 list the kings, princes, prophets, inhabitants of Jerusalem and the people of Judah as the devotees of the Host of Heaven and Jer. 44.17ff. similarly enumerates the people, their fathers, their kings and princes and the people of the land as the worshippers of the Queen of Heaven. But there are many such lists in the Jeremiah prose (e.g., 1.18; 17.20, 25; 19.3; 24.8; 25.18; 26.19–20; 29.1; 34.19; 37.2) and they often seem to be used with little other purpose than to suggest that *everyone* was implicated, from king to commoner. Thus 19.4 and 32.32 suggest that everyone in the land was in some way involved in the cult of the Hinnom Valley, but surely not that there was a national assembly in that place for the conduct of specific rites over which the king presided. Likewise, it is hardly to be deduced from 44.17, 21 that the Davidic king and his household were lighting fires and baking cakes for the Queen of Heaven in the villages of Judah and the streets of Jerusalem. These must be comprehensive phrases implying that everyone, even the king and his family, worshipped the Queen of Heaven everywhere, even in the city streets.

31. See the summary on p. 54. In this connection it is interesting to note that Caquot, *Syria* 36, p. 92, thinks of 'the cult of *ṣb'u.špš* as an element of popular religion in Ugarit'; but see further p. 50 and n. 56 below.

32. Grohmann, *Arabien*, pp. 81ff., 243ff.; but see also the comments by M. Höfner in *GMVO*, pp. 468–9.

33. E.g., the Moon-god was known as *Wadd, 'Almaqah, 'Amm, Sin, Hubal*; the Sun-goddess as *Nakrah, Šams, 'Athirat*; Venus mainly as *'Athtar* or *'Aśtar* and *Al-'Uzzā*. Some of the identifications are disputed; see *GMVO, in loc.*

34. Grohmann, *op. cit.*, p. 81.

35 G. Ryckmans, *Les religions arabes préislamiques*, Bibliothèque du Muséon 26, Louvain 1951, p. 41.

36. J. Gray, *JNES* 8, pp. 72–83 (see ch. V, n. 105). But contrast J. Henninger, 'Ist der sogenannte Nilus-Bericht eine brauchbare religionsgeschichtliche Quelle?', *Anthropos* 50, 1955, pp. 81–148, who feels that this late source shows little knowledge of bedouin life or religion.

37. Gurney, *op. cit.*, p. 139.

38. *Ibid.*, pp. 134–5.

39. *GMVO*, pp. 196–201.

40. *GMVO*, pp. 187–8; *ANET*, p. 120; E. Laroche, 'Divinités lunaires d'Anatolie', *RHR* 148, 1955, pp. 1–24. Laroche points out that these gods appear mostly in texts used in magic, divination, oaths, prophylactic acts, etc., and therefore belong to the religion of local superstition.

41. *GMVO*, pp. 179–80.

42. *GMVO*, pp. 340–2.

43. *GMVO*, pp. 389–93.

44. *GMVO*, pp. 331–3.

45. *GMVO*, pp. 402–3; F. W. Read, *Egyptian Religion and Ethics*, London 1925, p. 25.

46. J. A. Wilson, 'Egypt', in H. Frankfort and others, *Before Philosophy. The Intellectual Adventure of Ancient Man*, Pelican Books 1949, p. 56; C. Aldred, *The Egyptians*, Ancient Peoples and Places, London 1961, pp. 69, 107.

47. Caquot, *Syria* 36, pp. 90–101.

48. Gordon, *BASOR* 65, pp. 29–33; Gaster, *JRAS* 1938, pp. 37–56.

49. T. H. Gaster, 'A Canaanite Ritual Drama', *JAOS* 66, 1946, pp. 49–76.

50. Caquot, *Syria* 35, pp. 45–60.

51. See the discussion in Caquot, *Syria* 35, pp. 52–3, and McKay, *VT* 20, pp. 451–64. Both gods attempt to ascend the throne of the divine king and both are compelled to descend (*CML*, B III i. 25–37 = *CTCA*, 6 I 53–65).

52. *yd't.hlk.kbkbm*; *CML*, A I ii. 3, 7; iv. 38 = *CTCA*, 19.52, 56, 200.

53. *UT* 143; Virolleaud, *Syria* 28, p. 25; Sawyer and Stephenson, *art. cit.*

54. *CML*, K II i. 36; III v. 19; A I iv. 47 = *CTCA*, 16.36; 15 V. 19; 19.209; also *CTCA*, 35.47, 53.

55. Caquot, *Syria* 36, p. 92, n. 2.

56. For the translation 'host of the Sun', see Caquot, *Syria* 36, p. 91, n. 1; Gray, *JNES* 8, pp. 72ff.; C. H. Gordon, *Ugaritic Handbook*, AnOr 25, 1947, p. 264. But Driver, *CML*, p. 150, n. 29, relates *ṣb'* in this phrase to the Arabic *ḍaba'a* (concealed) and translates the phrase 'sunset'. Gordon has now accepted this translation (*UT*, p. 472). In K II i. 36; III v. 19; A I iv. 47 the phrase seems to be used as a time indicator, and in the last two of these passages stands in parallel to *'rb.špš*, 'the setting of the Sun'. In the first text there appears, however, to be some connection with 'the light of the countless (stars)', *nyr.rbt*. In *CTCA*, 35.47, 53, a ritual text listing sacrifices to various gods according to the days of a certain month, the phrase could refer either to the time of day when sacrifice is to be offered, i.e., at sunset, or to the celestial host for whom the offerings are made. Thus, whilst it is tempting to translate the phrase 'host of the Sun', it is certainly possible that Driver's suggestion is the correct one.

57. *CML*, S ii. 20 = *CTCA*, 23.54; cf. *CML*, A I iv. 31 = *CTCA*, 19.193.

58. Cf. Caquot, *Syria* 36, p. 92, n. 2.

59. I Kings 22.19. But it is by no means obvious that the Host of Heaven in this context includes the stars. However, see p. 57.

60. Judg. 16.23; I Sam. 5.2ff.; I Chron. 10.10; II Kings 1.2ff.

61. Herodotus, *Historiae* i. 105 (5th cent. BC).

62. R. A. S. Macalister, *The Philistines, their history and civilization*, Schweich Lectures 1911, London 1913, pp. 93ff.

63. Pauly-Wissowa 1, cols. 2763, 2772.

64. A. H. van Zyl, *The Moabites*, Pretoria Oriental Series 3, Leiden 1960, p. 181. Jensen, *ZA* 42, pp. 235–7, suggests a link with an Assyrian god *Kammuš*, identified with Nergal. But the name should be read *Kamsir*, not *Kammuš*.

65. Related to the Arabian Athtar? Cf. Gray, *JNES* 8, pp. 72–83. The composite name on the stone, Ashtar-Kemosh, possibly indicates that the two gods could be identified, suggesting an astral aspect in Kemosh also.

66. See ch. V, n. 106. For the *Balu'a* stele, see *ANEP*, Pl. 488.

67. Van Zyl, *op. cit.*, p. 195.

68. *GMVO*, p. 428; Gray, *JNES* 8, pp. 72–83.

69. T. H. Gaster, *Thespis. Ritual, Myth and Drama in the Ancient Near East*², Doubleday Anchor Books, New York 1961, p. 412.

70. Du Mesnil du Buisson, *RHR* 164, pp. 144f.

71. Eusebius, *Praeparatio Evangelica* I 10.32. In conjunction with this detail, Philo gives the tradition that Astarte, 'while she was travelling around the world, found a star which had fallen from the sky, and she took it up and consecrated it in the holy island of Tyre' (31). On the philological problems involved in the equation of Ishtar, Ashtart, Athtar, etc., see J. Mauchline, 'Ishtar – 'Ashtart', *TGUOS* 10, pp. 11–20.

72. Cicero, *De Natura Deorum* III.42 (1st cent. BC); Athenaeus, *Dipnosophistae* IX.392 (2nd–3rd cent. AD).

73. Morgenstern, *The Fire upon the Altar*, pp. 102–13; but see the comments by S. H. Hooke referred to in ch. III, n. 25.

74. See pp. 32f. For the possibility that Reshef was associated with some star or planet in Syria-Palestine, see Sawyer and Stephenson, *art. cit.*

75. See p. 30.

76. Dussaud, *Religions des hittites* . . ., pp. 396–9.

77. *Ibid.*, p. 399.

78. There have been a number of studies dealing with this topic, not all of the same value. Some have been extravagant and others fairly cautious, but all have added weight to the general impression that Israel did have a solar mythology and religion. C. V. L. Charlier, 'Ein astronomischer Beitrag zur Exegese der alten Testament', *ZDMG* 58, 1904, pp. 386–94, suggested, and sometimes his arguments are rather far-fetched, that underlying many of the ancient laws and much of the cultic terminology was an equinoctial solar festival. In the same vein is the work of Morgenstern, who in *HUCA* 6 and *The Fire upon the Altar* argued that the New Year Festival was originally the festival of a solar Yahweh. Similar conclusions were upheld by Hollis in his article in *Myth and Ritual*; he considered that the eastward orientation of the Temple and its relation to the Mount of Olives were indications of solar aspects in Jerusalemite religion. May, *ZAW* 55, even attempted to compile a history of Sun-worship in Palestine and reconstructed a mythology based on the battle between the seasons of summer and winter, in which the solstices quite naturally play a more important part than the equinoxes. A. F. von Gall, 'Ein neues astronomisch zu erschliessendes Datum der ältesten israelitischen Geschichte', *Beiträge zur alttestamentlichen Wissenschaft. Karl Budde zum 70. Geburtstag*, ed. K. Marti, BZAW 34, 1920, pp. 52–60, thought that Solomon's prayer of dedication betrays solar motifs drawn from the myth of the Sun's victory over the dragon of the eclipse. Schaeffer, *Ras Shamra—Ugarit*, p. 62, believes that the *šᵉbisim* in Isa. 3.18 are solar pendants similar to those found at Ras Shamra (see further pp. 54f. and n. 93 below; also fig. 17). H. St. J. Thackeray, 'New Light on the Book of Jashar', *JTS* 11 1909–11, pp. 518–32, maintained that solar mythology was contained in the Book of Jashar. C. F. Burney, *The Book of Judges*, London 1918, pp. 391–408, presents the view that a solar mythology underlies the Samson stories. A. R. Johnson, 'The Role of the King in the Jerusalem Cultus', *The Labyrinth. Further studies*

in the relation between myth and ritual in the ancient world, ed. S. H. Hooke, London, 1935, pp. 71–111, ref. pp. 81–3, thinks that El-Elyon, the god of Jebusite Jerusalem, was a Sun-god and that Yahweh took over much of this pre-Israelite solar mythology. If these works are approached with a little caution, there is much that is of value to be extracted from them, and if this information is taken together with that already presented (pp. 15f., 32ff., 37f.) a substantial picture begins to be formed.

79. Y. Aharoni, *The Land of the Bible: a historical geography*, ET, London 1967, p. 346. See fig. 13 below.

80. For criticism of Aharoni's arguments and for a summary of the views of W. F. Albright, D. Diringer, P. W. Lapp and F. M. Cross, all of whom date the two-winged stamp in Josiah's reign, see Lance, *HTR* 64; Tushingham, *BASOR* 201, pp. 23–25. Although it is generally agreed that the four-winged scarab stamps are older, it seems unlikely that they are as old as Aharoni maintains; cf. Lance, *art. cit.*, pp. 315f.

81. A. R. Millard, 'An Israelite Royal Seal?', *BASOR* 207, Dec. 1972, forthcoming.

82. See ch. V, n. 55. See also Tushingham, *art. cit.* (Part One), *BASOR* 200, 1970, pp. 71–8, ref. pp. 75f.

83. It has not always been the opinion of scholars that the two-winged figure is a Sun-disc. One view is that it symbolizes a flying scroll (cf. Zech. 5.1f.) and is to be associated with Josiah's reforming policies which were based on the scroll of the law (D. Diringer, 'The Royal Jar-Handle Stamps of Ancient Judah', *BA* 12, 1949, pp. 70–86; cf. his comments in Tufnell, *Lachish III*, pp. 342–4). It has also been argued that it often resembles a crested bird (C. C. McCown, *Tell en-Naṣbeh excavated under the direction of the late William Frederic Badè* I, The Palestine Institute of Pacific School of Religion and the American Schools of Oriental Research, Berkeley, 1947, p. 156). But the majority of scholars now accept that it is a winged Sun-disc (cf. Tushingham, *art. cit.* [Part Two], pp. 26ff.).

84. From Ras Shamra, cf. Schaeffer, *op. cit.*, Pl. XXXII.1 and p. 62; from Gezer, cf. Macalister, *Gezer* III, Pl. XXXI.13, 25; CCXXI.25; from Hazor, cf. Yadin and others, *Hazor III–IV*, Pl. CCCXLIII.28–36. See also fig. 14 below.

85. Yᵉrîḥō may be formed from the word yārēaḥ (the Moon); cf. A. Lods, *Israel from its beginnings to the middle of the eighth century*, ET, London 1953, p. 129; T. H. Gaster, 'Moon', *IDB* III, p. 436.

86. Yāraḥ (Gen. 10.26; I Chron. 1.20) and Yārōaḥ (I Chron. 5.14) may be formed from yārēaḥ; Ḥōdeš (I Chron. 8.9) means 'New Moon' precisely.

87. The texts cited by S. H. Langdon, *Babylonian Menologies and the Semitic Calendars*, Schweich Lectures 1933, London 1935, p. 77, suggest the possibility of similar beliefs in certain circles in Mesopotamia, for on the fourteenth and fifteenth of Nisan, when the Moon begins to wane, 'if one works he will lose his money' and 'one may not take oath nor transact business'.

88. It has recently been argued that the New Moon festival was never associated with lunar religion. Firstly, it is maintained that the Hebrew New Moon (ḥōdeš) was identical with our Full Moon. Hence it is argued that, since the light of Full Moon makes the night of its appearance a most suitable time for holding all night celebrations, the association of festivals with the ḥōdeš

has no religious significance; it is simply an appropriate calendrical arrange-ment. So N. H. Snaith, *The Jewish New Year Festival, its origins and development*, London, 1947, pp. 96ff.; A. Caquot, 'Remarques sur la fête de la néoménie dans l'ancien Israël', *RHR* 158, 1960, pp. 1–18; M. Petit, 'La lune en Canaan et Israël', *La lune, mythes et rites*, Sources Orientales 5, Éditions du Seuil, Paris 1962, pp. 129–50. But this theory depends on questionable premisses. Firstly, either it demands the equation of *ḥōdeš* with *kēseh* in Ps. 81.4, although the two are distinguished in a Phoenician inscription from Larnax Lapethos (*KAI* 43.12: [*bḥd*]*šm wbks'm yrḥ*; the absence of *wāw* in Ps. 81.4 is not therefore a sign of synonymity), or else it implies that *ḥōdeš* is the Full Moon and *kēseh* is not (this alternative has not been proposed, as far as I am aware). Secondly, it requires the premiss that Passover was a Full Moon festival, but with this I cannot agree (J. W. McKay, 'The Date of Passover and its Significance', *ZAW* 84, 1972, pp. 435–47). The *ḥōdeš* was hardly therefore important only because it was the night when the Moon's light was brightest; it must also have had religious significance.

89. Cf. the importance of the Moon to the Arabs whose caravans travelled mostly by night (T. J. Meek, 'The Sabbath in the Old Testament, its origin and development', *JBL* 33, 1914, pp. 201–12; W. O. E. Oesterley and T. H. Robinson, *Hebrew Religion, its origin and development*, London 1930, p. 128).

90. See pp. 9f., 23, 24, 30, 36f., 38f., 41, 42, 45–7.

91. L. H. Vincent, 'Les fouilles de Teleilat Ghassoul', *RB* 44, 1935, pp. 69–104, ref. pp. 102–4 and Pl. IV.2. See fig. 15 below.

92. R. A. S. Macalister, *Gezer* II, p. 349, figs. 465, 466. At first the symbols on this tablet were thought to represent the signs of the Zodiac, but it is now recognized that the Zodiac was not invented till much later (see p. 38). However, it may still be possible to maintain that some of the figures do represent stars and constellations. See the report, 'The Zodiacal Tablet', by R. A. S. Macalister in *PEFQS* 1907, pp. 245, 262ff., and the discussion in *PEFQS* 1908, by C. J. Ball (p. 26), C. H. W. Johns (p. 27), T. G. Pinches (p. 28), A. H. Sayce (p. 29), G. St. Clair (p. 78), R. A. S. Macalister (p. 208). See fig. 16 below.

93. O. Tufnell and others, *Lachish II*, Pl. XXVI.9–15 and p. 66; W. M. F. Petrie, *Ancient Gaza, Tell el Ajjūl*, Publications of the Egyptian Research Account and the British School of Archaeology in Egypt 53–6, London 1931–4, vol. III, Pls. VII and VIII; Schaeffer, *op. cit.*, Pl. XXXII.1 (but Schaeffer believes that the examples from Ras Shamra may be Sun-pendants; see n. 78 above). See fig. 17 below.

94. See p. 46 and figs. 8, 7, 9 below.

95. *ANEP*, Pl. 792. See fig. 18 below.

96. May, *Megiddo*, pp. 35–6; Gaster, *JRAS* 1938, pp. 40–1.

97. Petrie, *Ancient Gaza* I, Pl. XXVIII.4. Petrie (p. 10) thought that this pottery fragment was not of Palestinian origin, but Engberg (May, *Megiddo*, pp. 40–1) maintains that it is. See fig. 19 below.

98. Various stamps and seals with a stylized pentagram, cf. Macalister, *Gezer* II, p. 209, fig. 359; *idem*, *Gezer* III, Pl. CC.36; Bliss and Macalister, *Excavations*, Pl. 56.44z. Scratchings of stars on pottery, cf. Macalister, *Gezer* III, Pl. CXC.59; possibly Graham and May, *Culture and Conscience*, p. 39, fig. 5.

Stars used as filling on seals, cf. Macalister, *Gezer* II, p. 296, fig. 438; *idem*, *Gezer* III, Pl. ccviii.20. (For some of these see fig. 20 below.)

99. For the definitions of Babylonian star-names accepted here, see Weidner, *RA* III, pp. 72–82, and Gössmann, *Planetarium Babylonicum*. On problems of identification, see Gössmann. The identifications and translations of the Hebrew star-names are drawn from the writings of G. R. Driver (*art. cit.*, *JTS* NS 4, pp. 208–12 and NS 7, pp. 1–11) and of the Italian astronomer, G. V. Schiaparelli, but many different proposals have been made for the identification of each of the stars and constellations mentioned; see further the literature cited in ch. V, n. 79. but particularly Schiaparelli, ch. 4, where the different identifications are discussed in some detail. Despite the many uncertainties, and even though some of the identifications accepted here may prove finally unacceptable, I feel that it is legitimate to make the comparisons, partly because they illustrate differences rather than similarities. Indeed, it is significant that, in the various studies of the Hebrew star-names, little attempt has been made to find correspondences with Mesopotamian names. Perhaps the present outline discussion gives some indication why this should be.

100. The emendations necessary to obtain these identifications were proposed by G. Hoffmann, 'Versuche zu Amos', *ZAW* 3, 1883, pp. 87–126, ref. pp. 110–11, and are accepted by G. R. Driver, 'Stars', *HDB*[2], pp. 936–8.

101. Cf. Aratus, *Phaenomena* 167ff., 156ff., 137ff.

102. Schiaparelli suggests the group composed of Argo, Crux and Centaurus, but Driver thinks of two different star groups. He identifies *ḥeder* with the Southern Cross and *ḥadrē tēmān* with the Babylonian 'Way of Ea', i.e., the belt composed of Hydrus, Crater, Corvus, Procyon, Orion, Canicula, Lepus, Eridanus, Centaurus, Argo, Pisces and Ara.

103. See p. 39.

104. C. F. Burney, 'The Three Serpents of Is. 27.1', *JTS* 11, 1909–11, pp. 443–7; cf. C. Rabin, 'BĀRIAḤ', *JTS* 47, 1946, pp. 38–41, who suggests that *nāḥāš bārīaḥ* may have been Draco.

105. *CML*, B I* i.1–2 = *CTCA*, 5 I.1–2.

106. For this translation, see G. R. Driver, *HDB*[2], pp. 936–8; so also NEB.

107. But the precise significance of the mythological language in these verses is uncertain and the text need imply nothing more than an angelic appearance. See further the discussion by K. Galling, *art. cit.*, pp. 143f.

108. For the older opinion that Isa. 14.12–15 is based on a Mesopotamian original, see J. Skinner, *The Book of the Prophet Isaiah, Chapters I–XXXIX*, CBSC, 1896, p. 122; G. W. Wade, *The Book of the Prophet Isaiah*, WC, 1911, pp. 100–1; G. B. Gray, *A Critical and Exegetical Commentary on the Book of Isaiah, I–XXVII*, ICC, 1912, pp. 225–6; H. Günkel, *Schöpfung und Chaos in Urzeit und Endzeit. Eine religionsgeschichtliche Untersuchung über Gen. 1 und Ap. Joh. 12*, Göttingen 1895, p. 132.

109. Snaith, *The Jewish New Year Festival*, p. 97, identifies as 'New Moon-god, son of the Moon-god' (cf. D. Winton Thomas, *Liber Jesaiae*, BHS, 1968, *ad loc.*). H. G. May, *ZAW* 55, suggests that Shahar was the Sun at winter solstice and Helel the Sun at summer solstice. G. R. Driver, *HDB*[2], pp. 936–8, maintains that Helel was the royal star, Jupiter-Marduk. But none of these suggestions takes into consideration the use of the term *šaḥar* in the rest of

the Old Testament where it does mean 'dawn'. For a fuller assessment of these and other arguments and for my own opinion that Helel is Venus as the morning star and that Shahar is the goddess of the dawn, see *VT* 20, pp. 451–64.

110. In *VT* 20, pp. 451–64, I argued that Isa. 14.12–15 is dependent on the Greek myth which came to Palestine through Phoenician mediation. It may, however, also be possible to think of a Semitic, or perhaps common Eastern Mediterranean original which has found its way into Greek mythology. I can find no means of giving a final judgment on this, but in general terms, probably because of the spread of Semitic culture in the Mediterranean through the Phoenician traders, Greek mythology owes more to Semitic influence than early Semitic mythology to Greek, and it may be more appropriate to set the Helel/Phaethon myth against this wider background.

111. So, for example, W. Rudolph, *Jeremia*[3], HAT 12, 1968, p.73; A. Weiser, *Das Buch Jeremia*[5], ATD 20/21, 1966, p.87; A. Aeschimann, *Le prophète Jérémie. Commentaire*, Paris 1959, p.90.

112. 'The customs': lit. 'the way' (*derek*); 'even though': lit. 'because' (*kî*). For the translation here, see Rudolph, *Jeremia*, p.70; Bright, *Jeremiah*, p.78.

113. See *CAD*, vol.I–J, pp.306–8.

114. For a fairly full discussion of this kind of religious fear, see M. Eliade, *Patterns in Comparative Religion*, ET, London and New York 1958, ch.II.

115. *'ōnēn*, to practise soothsaying by observation of the clouds (cf. *'ānān*, a cloud): II Kings 21.6; II Chron. 33.6; Deut. 18.10; Lev. 19.26 (H); Isa. 2.6; Jer. 27.9; Micah 5.11, EVV 12; Judg. 9.37.

niḥēš, to divine by snake charming (cf. *nāḥāš*, a serpent): II Kings 21.6; II Chron. 33.6; II Kings 17.17; Deut. 18.10; Num. 23.23; 24.1 (both JE).

qāsam, to divine with arrows (cf. Arabic *qasama*, to divide, distribute; *'istaqsama* is used of procuring a divine decision by drawing lots with headless arrows): Deut. 18.10; Isa. 3.2; Jer. 14.14; Num. 22.7; 23.23 (both JE); I Sam. 15.23.

kiššēp, to practise sorcery (cf. Accadian *kaššāpu*, a sorcerer): Deut. 18.10; II Chron. 33.6; II Kings 9.22; Micah 5.11; Ex. 22.17.

'ōb, necromancy (the witch of Endor was an *'ēšet ba'alat-'ōb*): II Kings 21.6; 23.24; II Chron. 33.6; Deut. 18.11; Isa. 8.19; I Sam. 28.3, 9; I Chron. 10.13.

yiddeʿōnî, necromancy (difficult to distinguish from *'ōb*): II Kings 21.6; 23.24; II Chron. 33.6; Deut. 18.11; Isa. 8.19; 19.3; I Sam. 28.3ff.

Most of these definitions have been subject to debate at one time or another. On these and other types of divination in early Israel, see S. R. Driver, *A Critical and Exegetical Commentary on the Book of Deuteronomy*[3], ICC, 1902 pp.223–6; Montgomery, *Kings*, p.520; Gray, *Kings*, pp.648–9, 707; E. Dhorme, 'Prêtres, devins et mages dans l'ancienne religion des hébreux', *RHR* 108, 1933, pp.113–43; *idem*, *L'évolution religieuse d'Israel* I, *La religion des hébreux nomades*, Série de l'Orient Ancien de l'Institut de philologie et d' histoires orientales et slaves de l'Université de Bruxelles, Brussels 1937, pp.229ff. Apart from the observation that most of these practices were current in Israel before the Assyrians came, it may also be noted that similar divinatory methods were widespread in the ancient Near East, particularly amongst the Arabian tribes (Driver, *loc. cit.*).

116. In addition to the material cited in this chapter the following three studies are of interest, although they must be read with some caution. R. A. Rosenberg, 'The God Ṣedeq', *HUCA* 36, 1965, pp. 161–77, argues that the Jebusite god Ṣedeq was a solar deity; J. B. Curtis, *art. cit.*, suggests that Shalim was worshipped as Saturn in Jerusalem and that the Mount of Olives was the seat of a cult of Nergal, who is associated with Mars; H. Lewy, 'The Origin and Significance of the Magen Dawid', *AO* 18.2, 1950, pp. 330–65, also maintains that the cult of Shalim-Saturn was indigenous in Jerusalem.

117. See p. 50.

118. The cult of the Host of Heaven flourished in the Jerusalem Temple particularly during the reign of Manasseh (II Kings 21.5) and was suppressed by Josiah (II Kings 23.4).

119. This is certainly the reason given by devotees of the Queen of Heaven for their worship of that goddess (Jer. 44.15–23). See further p. 11 and ch. II, n. 51.

CHAPTER VII

1. A good outline of the Assyrian religio-political ideal in similar terms to these is given by H. Schmökel in H. Schmökel and others, *Mesopotamien, Hethiterreich, Syrien-Palästina, Urartu*, Kulturgeschichte des alten Orient, Stuttgart, 1961, pp. 99–100; W. von Soden, 'Religion und Sittlichkeit nach den Anschauungen der Babylonier', *ZDMG* NF 14, 1935, pp. 143–69, ref. p. 152; K. Tallqvist, *Der assyrische Gott*, pp. 93–105; G. van Driel, *The Cult of Aššur*, pp. 190–1.

2. Neither Schmökel, von Soden, Tallqvist, nor van Driel venture as far as this.

3. Gressmann, *art. cit.*, p. 324. Gressmann appeals to the series of source references collected by M. Streck, *Assurbanipal* I, p. cccxl, n. 3.

4. Streck, *Assurbanipal* II, p. 41. For Bêlit, read Ninlil; see ch. V, n. 6.

5. Streck, *Assurbanipal* I, p. cccxl, n. 3.

6. Cyrus of Persia appears to have restored or permitted the restoration of gods and cultic apparatus taken by the Babylonians: *ANET*, p. 316; Ezra 6.3–5.

7. When Ashurbanipal came to Susa he found there a statue of Nanai of Erech; D. D. Luckenbill, *Ancient Records of Assyria and Babylonia*, Chicago, 1926–7, vol. II, p. 311.

8. After the battle of Aphek the Philistines took the captured ark to the temple of Dagon in Ashdod; I Sam. 5.1ff.

9. After the capture of Rabbah, David took the crown from the head of the Ammonite god, Milkom; II Sam. 12.30; I Chron. 20.2 (pointing *milkōm* with LXX of both and Vg of I Chron. 20.2; but MT pointing *malkām*, 'their king', may be more correct; see further ch. V, n. 105.

10. E.g., Tiglath-pileser I, *Prism Inscription*, col. II, line 31 (Luckenbill, *Ancient Records* I, p. 75): 'His wives, his sons, the offspring of his loins, his

household, 180 vessels of bronze, 5 bowls of copper, together with their gods, gold and silver, the choicest of their possessions, I carried away.'

11. The text reads thus: *sattukkī^{meš} gi-né-e* SAG^{meš} *aššur(an.šár) u ^dnin-líl u ilāni^{meš} māt aššur(an.šár)^{ki} ú-kin ṣēru(edin)-uš-šú-un.* (Ashurbanipal, *Annals* [*Rassam Cylinder*], col.IV, lines 106–7.) Streck, *Assurbanipal* II, p.41, translates: 'Die vormaligen (?), feststehenden und regelmässigen Opfer für Aššur, Bêlit und die grossen Gottheiten Assyriens trug ich ihnen auf.' This is the translation accepted by Gressmann, *loc. cit.*, and used by him as the basis for his argument that the worship of Ashur was reimposed in Babylon. But Luckenbill, *Ancient Records* II, p.305, translates: 'Revenues, dues and firstfruits (?) for Assur and Bêlit, and the gods of Assyria, I imposed upon them'; and his translation suggests a demand for a financial contribution to the Assyrian state religion rather than a reimposition of an abandoned cult. W. G. Lambert has written to me on these lines as follows: 'The problem is how to read the ideogram SAG, and while I cannot prove one meaning correct, I consider "former" the least likely rendering. "First quality" as an adjective is possible, or "the choicest things" (a noun) in apposition to the two preceding words for "regular offering" may also be right. "First fruits" I would reject.' Thus either of two translations seem acceptable: 'regular offerings of the first quality' or 'regular offerings, the choicest things'. Neither translation alters the meaning of the text or prejudices the present discussion.

12. Cf. the references collected by van Driel, *op. cit.*, pp.190–1. Even the phrase *sattukū ginû* is used by Esarhaddon in his record of the burden laid on Egypt. Note also that van Driel's assessment of the significance of these records is in accord with that given here.

13. A. T. Olmstead, *History of Assyria*, New York—London 1923, p.617.

14. It may even be that some form of Assyrian cult existed in Babylon under royal patronage, for according to the *Synchronistic Chronicle* (*ANET*, pp.272–4), Sennacherib, Esarhaddon and Ashurbanipal all ruled both Assyria and Babylon, and latterly the Babylonian throne was delegated to Ashurbanipal's brother, Shamash-shum-ukin. Hence the cult of Ashur, Ninlil and the gods of Assyria may have been well established in Babylon under the patronage of Ashurbanipal's fathers, his brother and the Assyrian ruling officials before Shamash-shum-ukin's revolt. (Selections from Ashurbanipal's account of this revolt are given in *ANET*, pp.297ff.)

15. As noted by V. Korošec, *Hethitische Staatsverträge. Ein Beitrag zu ihrer juristischen Wertung*, Leipziger rechtswissenschaftliche Studien 60, Leipzig 1931, p.95; G. E. Mendenhall, 'Puppy and Lettuce in North-west Semitic Covenant Making', *BASOR* 133, 1954, pp.26–30, ref. p.30.

16. D. J. McCarthy, *Treaty and Covenant. A study in form in the ancient oriental documents and in the Old Testament*, AnBib 21, 1963, pp.197–8; *ANET*, pp.533–4.

17. Cf. McCarthy, *op. cit.*, p.79, n.36.

18. *ANET*, pp.532–3.

19. Cf. the god-list that introduces the treaty. For text and translation of VTE, see D. J. Wiseman, 'The Vassal-Treaties of Esarhaddon', *Iraq* 20, 1958, Part I. See also the critical apparatus and comments by R. Borger, 'Zu den

Asarhaddon-Verträgen aus Nimrud', *ZA* 54, 1961, pp. 173–96. Further translations are given by E. Reiner, 'Akkadian Treaties from Syria and Assyria', *ANET*, pp. 531–41, ref. pp. 534ff., and McCarthy, *op. cit.*, pp. 198–205.

20. As far as I have been able to ascertain, no one has yet appealed to these passages as evidence in the discussion, but it is possible that some would now wish to see in them positive support for the claims of Östreicher and his followers.

21. Reiner's translation. On this and Wiseman's translation, see below, n. 22.

22. Wiseman's translation (cf. also McCarthy's) gives a slightly different sense to the paragraph:

393 For the future and for ever Ashur is your god,
394 Ashurbanipal, the crown-prince, is your lord.
395 Your sons (and) your grandsons
396 will revere his sons.

Here the object of the verb 'revere' (Reiner translates 'fear') is not Ashur and Ashurbanipal, but Ashurbanipal's sons; cf. the similar demand for respect for the king's sons in the treaty between Ashurnirari V and Mati'ilu of Arpad (*ANET*, p. 533, sect. v). In this context lines 393–4 appear to serve a double function as a declaration of authority and as a sanction for fidelity. But once more there is no implication that the vassals were required to introduce the cult of Ashur to their native shrines. The paragraph, as Wiseman translates it, may be paraphrased in this way: 'Take this oath seriously and teach it to your children. You have sworn to recognize Ashurbanipal as crown-prince and your descendants must likewise hold his sons in reverence. If you fail in this duty, then beware. Remember that you are now subjects of Ashurbanipal and Ashur; they are your lords and masters.'

The difference between Wiseman's and Reiner's translations arises from the difficulty in reading line 396. The text is fragmentary, but Wiseman restores the words *a-na* DUMU.MEŠ-*šú* in this line. Reiner, however, prefers the reading *a-na* [*ša*]-*šú*. Borger, *art. cit.*, p. 186, drew attention to two texts, nos. 36 and 37, which offer . . .]x-*šú* and *a-na* [x]-*šú* respectively. 'Sons' would have to be written with two signs, DUMU.MEŠ, but no. 37 has room for one sign only. Nevertheless, whatever may be the correct original reading, the problem for the present study remains substantially the same, namely, to decide what is implied in the definition of Ashur as 'your god'. (I am indebted to W. G. Lambert for his comments on the translation of this difficult text.)

23. Cf. Wiseman, *op. cit.*, Pl. 6, 31. Because of its fragmentary nature, restoration is in part conjectural (*ibid.*, p. 86). But the text of the important lines. 407–9, is in better condition and its translation is not subject to the same doubt.

24. Each extant copy of the treaty bears three seals: the seal of Sennacherib, the seal of Ashur and a middle Assyrian royal seal (Wiseman, *op. cit.*, p. 14).

25. Reiner's translation. Wiseman's (cf. also McCarthy's) translation of lines 407–9 reads:

407 You will not make a claim against (a document bearing)

408 the seal of Ashur, king of the gods. It is set in your presence,
409 you will serve (him) as your own god.

Whilst there are differences between the readings and the translations of Reiner and Wiseman, these do not raise the same problems for our present investigation as did the differences in their interpretations of lines 393–6.

26. These conclusions from context are not affected by the fact that DINGIR (lines 393, 409) means 'god' and not 'overlord' (*CAD*, vol.I–J, pp.91ff.; Tallqvist, *Götterepitheta*, p.491). The language in VTE, it seems to me, is entirely comparable with that used in Ps. 2.10–12 (see p.64).

27. So BH³, RSV and many commentators; cf. W. O. E. Oesterley, *The Psalms translated with text-critical and exegetical notes*, London 1939, p.124; A. Weiser, *The Psalms, a commentary*, ET, OTL, 1962, p.109. MT reads. 'rejoice with trembling, kiss (the) son'. Few scholars find the MT acceptable, partly because the word translated 'son' is the Aramaic *bar*, and partly because it has so little support from the Versions. On the other hand, the translation accepted here is based on an entirely conjectural emendation, as also is NEB's 'tremble, and kiss the king'. However, the significance of these verses is clear. The kings and rulers are called upon to submit themselves to Yahweh as their overlord, perhaps demonstrating their loyalty before the king as Yahweh's representative. Cf. Oesterley, *op. cit.*, p. 126: 'By the words *serve Yahweh in fear* are meant "Be subject to me", *i.e.*, Yahweh's representative.' Possibly VTE 393, 409 are to be understood in this way, Ashurbanipal (394) being Ashur's representative.

28. McCarthy, *op. cit.*, p.78.

29. *Ibid.*, p.74.

30. Wiseman, *op. cit.*, p.4.

31. *Ibid.*, p.3.

32. Cf. M. Weinfeld, 'Traces of Assyrian Treaty Formulae in Deuteronomy', *Biblica* 46, 1965, pp.417–27; R. Frankena, 'The Vassal-Treaties of Esarhaddon and the Dating of Deuteronomy', OTS 14, 1965. pp.122–54. Manasseh's visit to Assyria to swear the oath may have been the event to which II Chron. 33.10–13 alludes, in which case Manasseh may have gone to Assyria in or soon after 672 BC, his fifteenth year on the throne. But the Chronicler obviously associated Manasseh's abduction with a time of unrest and it seems more likely that the visit to which he refers happened at a later date, certainly after the revolt of Egypt in 665 BC, and perhaps as late as the time of the Babylonian uprising in 652 BC. If this is correct (see further pp. 25f.), it may still be possible that Manasseh, when he did appear before the Assyrian king, was required to reaffirm his allegiance by taking the oath in VTE.

33. *ANET*. p.320.

34. *ANET*, pp.499–500.

35. *ANET*, pp.501–2.

36. See further, S. Mowinckel, *The Psalms in Israel's Worship*, ET, Oxford 1962, vol.I, p.55.

37. 'All the nations over whom my name has been called' (Amos 9.12) could be thought to imply that Israel did try, but the phrase seems to mean little more than 'all the nations which Israel once possessed (i.e., conquered

or ruled)'. Cf. II Sam. 12.28 where Joab tells David to take Rabbath-Ammon himself, 'lest I (Joab) take the city and my name be called over it'.

38. *KAI* 218.

39. Cf. Saggs, *op. cit.*, p.21, n.2, who cites an example from Sargon's *Annals* 99: 'I established the Weapon of Ašur as their deity'. Saggs himself, however, considers that this was not a regular practice amongst the Assyrians (see n.40 below).

W. G. Lambert has also drawn my attention to D. D. Luckenbill, *The Annals of Sennacherib*, The University of Chicago Oriental Institute Publications 2, Chicago, 1924, p.62, lines 87–91:

I restored Illubru again:
people of the lands which my hands had conquered I settled therein.
The weapon of Assur, my lord, I established in its midst.
An alabaster stela I had (them) fashion
and set up before him (Assur or the 'weapon' of Assur).

It appears that the word translated 'weapon' in both the above texts, *kakku*, refers to a symbol which served for the divine presence instead of the statue (*AHw*, p.422, see *kakku(m)* II.3). Although Sennacherib's text lacks the words 'as their deity', they would appear to be implied.

40. So also Saggs, *op. cit.*, p.21: 'Contemporary documents provide, however, no clear evidence of the regular enforcing of such a practice by the Assyrians.'

CHAPTER VIII

1. Both the translators of the Versions and modern commentators have had great difficulty with this verse. W. R. Harper, *A Critical and Exegetical Commentary on the Books of Amos and Hosea*, ICC, 1905, p.140, gives thirteen possible interpretations of this verse and still the debate continues; see recently S. Gevirtz, 'A New Look at an Old Crux: Am.5.26', *JBL* 87, 1968, pp.267–76. The proposal to find reference to Sakkuth and Kaiwan is, however, the most widely favoured and may be found discussed in most commentaries on Amos.

2. Tallqvist, *Götterepitheta*, pp.421, 440. On the association of Ninurta with Saturn, which does not appear to represent a primary aspect of the god, see *ibid.*, p.424; Gössmann, *Planetarium Babylonicum*, p.124.

3. Gössmann, *loc. cit.*

4. Cf. R. S. Cripps, *A Critical and Exegetical Commentary of the Book of Amos²*, London 1955, pp.300–2. But the suggestion that the oracle is editorial depends mainly on the supposition that Judah was obliged to worship Assyrian gods.

5. Some of these have already been discussed; see pp.16, 22f.

6. On the problem of dating, see ch.IV, n.27.

7. So J. P. Peters, 'The Worship of Tammuz', *JBL* 36, 1917, pp.100–11. But Albright, *JAOS* 60, pp.297–8, believes that Isaiah had a Syrian Adonis cult in mind (see ch.III, n.46); cf. R. de Vaux, *The Bible and the Ancient Near*

East, ET, London 1972, pp. 212f. For a discussion of the Tammuz cult in Ezek. 8, see G. A. Cooke, *A Critical and Exegetical Commentary on the Book of Ezekial,* ICC, 1936, pp.96–8; Zimmerli, *Ezechiel* I, pp.219–20, and bibliography there.

8. Commentators suggest *Zarpānītu,* the consort of Marduk, or *Sakkud,* or a non-existent composite deity, *Sakkud-Banītu.* See further, Montgomery, *Kings,* pp.473–4; Gray, *Kings,* p.654; de Vaux, *Rois,* p.203.

9. See p.48.

10. Ashima may be the Syrian god whose name appears in later Greek writings as Σίμι or Σείμιος and was identified with Mercury (see p.51). He is perhaps the god mentioned in Amos 8.14 and his name is possibly a component of *'šmbyt'l,* a deity known from Elephantine. Cf. Montgomery, *Kings,* p.475; Cripps, *Amos,* pp.316–7; E. König, 'Die Gottheit Aschima', *ZAW* 34, 1914, pp.19–30.

11. Cf. de Vaux, *Rois,* p.203. Although the identification of Awwa has been long debated and several localities have been suggested (see commentaries), the likelihood is that it is Awan, one of the three religious centres of Elam (so also de Vaux, *loc. cit.*; Šanda, *Könige* II, p.225; on the religious centres of Elam, see R. Labat, *Elam, c. 1600–1200 BC,* The Cambridge Ancient History[2] II.29, Cambridge, 1963, fasc.). In the god list *An = Anum,* in tablet VI, there is a section on Elamite gods. Here we find the names of seven Elamite gods, the second, third and fourth being *Ibnaḫaš.*[..], *Ibnasasa* (or *Ibnadidi?*) and *Daḫšešriš* (var. *Daḫšešra*). There follows another version of this list in which the third and fourth gods are named *Ibnaḫaza* and *Dakdadra* (identified as *ᵈe-[a],* the water god, and *ᵈ*EN.[ZU], the Moon god, respectively). See further, C. Frank, 'Elamische Götter', *ZA* 28, 1914, pp.323–9. Because of the differences between the two versions, the original forms of the names of the gods remain uncertain, but the similarities between the names in the second version and the Old Testament *nibḥaz* and *tartāq,* particularly since they occur in the same order, may suggest that it was a pair of Elamite gods that the settlers from Awwa brought to the land of Israel. For other suggestions, particularly that *nibḥaz* is a corruption of *mizbēaḥ* (altar) and that *tartāq* is the Syrian Atargatis/Derceto, see the commentaries, especially Montgomery, *Kings,* pp.474–5.

12. The first components of the god-names suggest the Mesopotamian deities Adad and Anu, whose names are probably here conflate with *mlk* the term (god?) used in connection with the Hinnom cult (see pp.39–41). Since child sacrifice appears to have been a feature of their worship, the composite nature of the names may well suggest some form of syncretism with West Semitic religion; cf. Gray, *Kings,* p.655 and see ch.V, n.98.

13. Some of the impressions conveyed in this summary, particularly those concerning the relationship between Josiah and the Deuteronomists, are based on my Ph.D. thesis. The present study, however, is not the correct place to set forth the somewhat detailed arguments that underlie these conclusions, but I hope that at some future date I may be able to present a fuller account of the age of Josiah in print. In the meantime, I offer these impressions merely to show that it is possible to find an alternative solution to the problem of Josiah's reforms. See also ch.V, n.110.

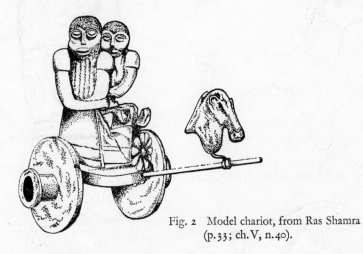

Fig. 1   Clay livers, from Gezer and Hazor (p. 8; ch. II, n. 26).

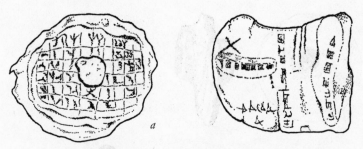

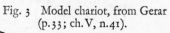

Fig. 2   Model chariot, from Ras Shamra
(p. 33; ch. V, n. 40).

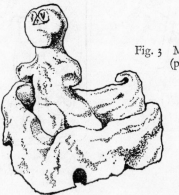

Fig. 3   Model chariot, from Gerar
(p. 33; ch. V, n. 41).

Fig. 4 Model wheels, from Megiddo (p. 33; ch. V, n. 42).

Fig. 5 Horse with disc on its forehead, from Jerusalem (p. 33; ch. V, n. 45).

Fig. 6 Horse's head with disc and cross, from Hazor (p. 33; ch. V, n. 46).

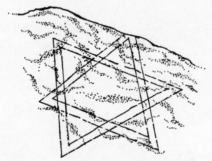

Fig. 7 Star on wall of the Anat temple at Megiddo (p. 46; ch. VI, n. 8).

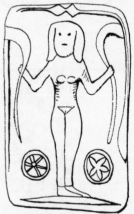

Fig. 8 Mother-goddess plaque, from *Tell eṣ-Ṣāfi* (p. 46; ch. VI, n. 9).

Fig. 9 Incense altar, from Gezer
(p. 46; ch. VI, n. 10).

Fig. 10 Lion attacking a gazelle
on a golden cup, from
Ras Shamra (ch. VI, n. 11).

Fig. 11 Mother-goddess plaque, from
Ras Shamra (p. 47; ch. VI, n. 15).

Fig. 12   Mother-goddesses holding raisin-cakes (?), from Gezer and Hazor
(ch. VI, n. 18).

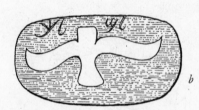

Fig. 13   *Lmlk* seals
(p. 52, ch. VI, n. 79).

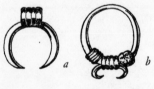

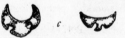

Fig. 14   Moon-pendants, from Ras Shamra
and Hazor, and figurine with Moon-pendant
attached to a neck-band, from Gezer
(p. 53; ch. VI, n. 84).

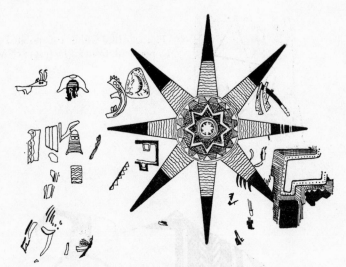

Fig. 15 Wall painting, from *Telēlāt Ghassūl* (p. 54; ch. VI, n. 91).

Fig. 16 Seal impression on the 'Zodiacal' tablet, from Gezer
(p. 54; ch. VI, n. 92).

 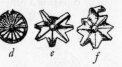

Fig. 17 Star pendants, from Lachish
and Ras Shamra (pp. 54 f.; ch. VI, n. 93).

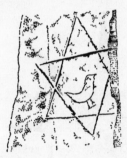

Fig. 18   Bird within a six-pointed star
on a potsherd, from *El-Jib* (p. 55; ch. VI, n. 95).

Fig. 19   Potsherd depicting a bird with a star on its wing, from ancient Gaza
(p. 55; ch. VI, n. 97).

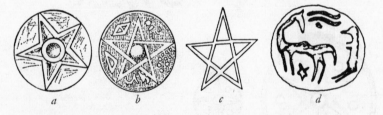

Fig. 20   Potters' stamps, pottery marking and a seal with animals and a star
(p. 55; ch. VI, n. 98).

INDEXES

1. AUTHORS AND WORKS CITED

Italic type indicates full bibliographical reference

2. SUBJECTS

(a) Gods and Astral Phenomena

(b) People and Places

(c) Linguistic, cultic and other subjects

3. BIBLICAL REFERENCES